WILDLIFE PROTECTION, DESTRUCTION AND EXTINCTION

THE LACEY ACT

FEDERAL REGULATION AND PROTECTION OF WILDLIFE AND PLANTS

WILDLIFE PROTECTION, DESTRUCTION AND EXTINCTION

Additional books in this series can be found on Nova's website under the Series tab.

Additional E-books in this series can be found on Nova's website under the E-book tab.

ENVIRONMENTAL SCIENCE, ENGINEERING AND TECHNOLOGY

Additional books in this series can be found on Nova's website under the Series tab.

Additional E-books in this series can be found on Nova's website under the E-book tab.

WILDLIFE PROTECTION, DESTRUCTION AND EXTINCTION

THE LACEY ACT

FEDERAL REGULATION AND PROTECTION OF WILDLIFE AND PLANTS

GILBERT E. MORGAN
AND
DEAVON HILL
EDITORS

Nova Science Publishers, Inc.
New York

Library of Congress Cataloging-in-Publication Data

ISBN: 978-1-62081-615-8

Published by Nova Science Publishers, Inc. † New York

CONTENTS

PREFACE

The Lacey Act was enacted in 1900 to prevent hunters from killing game in one state and escaping prosecution by crossing state lines. It has evolved into a law that prohibits import, export, transport, purchase, or sales of species when that action would violate state, federal, tribal or foreign law. Congress amended the Lacey Act most recently in 2008, expanding the reach of the act to include timber and timber products. It also regulated the introduction of non-native species and prohibited shipment of wildlife without clear identification of the contents and shipper. This book examines the Lacey Act, with a focus on protecting the environment by restricting trade; compliance issues related to importing plants and plant products; the Lacey Act Amendment; and Lacey Act Primer.

Chapter 1 - The Lacey Act was enacted in 1900 to prevent hunters from killing game in one state and escaping prosecution by crossing state lines. It has evolved into a law that prohibits import, export, transport, purchase, or sale of species when that action would violate state, federal, tribal, or foreign law. Congress amended the Lacey Act most recently in 2008, expanding the reach of the act to include timber and timber products. Implementation of the 2008 Amendments has proved controversial, and the Department of Agriculture Animal and Plant Health Inspection Service (APHIS) initially delayed implementing the act's new declaration requirements for importing wood products.

Some find the Lacey Act puzzling. While people charged with violating the act are charged with violating a US law, that prosecution is premised on a violation of another law, sometimes the law of another country. That has led some to claim that the United States is enforcing the laws of another country. US conservation laws (such as the Lacey Act), however, have long protected species and habitats even outside of the United States. Worldwide conservation was one reason for expanding Lacey Act coverage to more plants in 2008. Preserving US timber jobs and prices was another reason. However, the 2008 Amendments allow enforcement of foreign laws that are not directly related to conservation or US jobs, such as failure to pay foreign stumpage fees, or shipping wood in violation of a country's export restrictions. After search warrants were executed by the Department of the Interior Fish and Wildlife Service (FWS) against Gibson Guitar Corp. of Nashville, TN, apparently based on the possible illegal import of wood from India, Congress has taken another look at whether the 2008 Amendments achieve the goals of the Lacey Act. As introduced in October 2011, H.R. 3210 would amend the act to limit its application to wood imported prior to 2008 and composite wood products, and would allow an innocent owner defense to forfeiture actions. A different approach is taken by S. 2062, which would eliminate any reference to violations of foreign laws and end criminal prosecutions for violating the act.

Chapter 2 - The Lacey Act regulates the trade of wildlife and plants and creates penalties for a broad spectrum of violations. In 2008, the Lacey Act was amended to include protections for foreign plants and to require adherence to foreign laws as they pertain to certain conservation and other activities involving plants. Further, the 2008 amendments make it unlawful to submit falsified documents related to any plant or plant product covered by the act, and to import certain plant and plant products without an import declaration.

The primary drivers behind the Lacey Act amendments of 2008 (2008 amendments) were to reduce illegal logging globally and increase the value of US wood exports. Illegal logging is a pervasive problem with economic and environmental consequences. The World Bank estimates that illegal logging costs governments approximately $5 billion annually in lost royalties and an additional $10 billion in lost revenue. Further, if there were no illegally logged wood in the global market, it has been projected that the value of US exports of roundwood, sawnwood, and panels could increase by an average of approximately $460 million each year. A halt to illegal logging would also raise the value of domestic wood production. If this is added to exports, the estimated increase in revenue for companies in the United States could be approximately $1.0 billion annually.

A highly publicized raid on Gibson Guitar Corporation brought to light several existing policy issues related to the 2008 amendments to the Lacey Act. Some issues are broad and address the intent of the act. For example, some question why US importers should be held responsible for violations of foreign law or if the requirements under the Lacey Act actually reduce illegal logging. Other issues are narrow and address certain requirements in the act. For example, several suggest that the declaration requirements for importing plant and plant products are cumbersome and not possible to meet in some cases. Further, some contend that the 2008 amendments should not apply to plants harvested or plant products fabricated before the 2008 amendments were enacted. Countering these arguments are those that reiterate the benefits of the 2008 amendments, primarily reducing illegal logging and increasing the economic value of legally obtained plants and plant products on the market.

Congress is addressing these issues through proposed legislation. H.R. 3210 (The Retailers and Entertainers Lacey Implementation and Enforcement Fairness Act; RELIEF Act) was introduced on October 14, 2011, and addresses issues related to declaration requirements, penalties, reporting requirements, and certification standards, among other things authorized under the Lacey Act. Efforts to address implementation issues are also being pursued through regulations. The Animal and Plant Health Inspection Service (APHIS) is soliciting comments on regulatory options that can address issues related to declaration requirements, and is expected to release a report evaluating the implementation of declaration standards under the 2008 amendments.

Chapter 3 - The Lacey Act amendments included in the 2008 Farm Bill were effective as of May 22, 2008. As a practical matter, this means that enforcement actions may be taken for any violations committed on or after that date. The requirement to provide a declaration under the amended Act went into effect May 1, 2009.

The most recent phase of the implementation began April1, 2010, at which point all products on the revised schedule require a declaration. To view the phase-in schedule, see: http://www.aphis.usda.gov/plant health/lacey act/ downloads/ImplementationSchedule.pdf.

Chapter 4 – The Purpose of the Lacey Act Amendment is 1) to prevent trade in illegally harvested lumber; 2) to prevent trade in wood products made from illegally harvested lumber.

In: The Lacey Act
Editors: G. E. Morgan and D. Hill

ISBN 978-1-62081-615-8

Chapter 1

THE LACEY ACT: PROTECTING THE ENVIRONMENT BY RESTRICTING TRADE*

Kristina Alexander

SUMMARY

The Lacey Act was enacted in 1900 to prevent hunters from killing game in one state and escaping prosecution by crossing state lines. It has evolved into a law that prohibits import, export, transport, purchase, or sale of species when that action would violate state, federal, tribal, or foreign law. Congress amended the Lacey Act most recently in 2008, expanding the reach of the act to include timber and timber products. Implementation of the 2008 Amendments has proved controversial, and the Department of Agriculture Animal and Plant Health Inspection Service (APHIS) initially delayed implementing the act's new declaration requirements for importing wood products.

Some find the Lacey Act puzzling. While people charged with violating the act are charged with violating a US law, that prosecution is premised on a violation of another law, sometimes the law of another country. That has led some to claim that the United States is enforcing the laws of another country. US conservation laws (such as the Lacey Act),

---

* This is an edited, reformatted and augmented version of a Congressional Research Service publication, CRS Report for Congress R42067, from www.crs.gov, prepared for Members and Committees of Congress, dated February 16, 2012.

however, have long protected species and habitats even outside of the United States. Worldwide conservation was one reason for expanding Lacey Act coverage to more plants in 2008. Preserving US timber jobs and prices was another reason. However, the 2008 Amendments allow enforcement of foreign laws that are not directly related to conservation or US jobs, such as failure to pay foreign stumpage fees, or shipping wood in violation of a country's export restrictions. After search warrants were executed by the Department of the Interior Fish and Wildlife Service (FWS) against Gibson Guitar Corp. of Nashville, TN, apparently based on the possible illegal import of wood from India, Congress has taken another look at whether the 2008 Amendments achieve the goals of the Lacey Act. As introduced in October 2011, H.R. 3210 would amend the act to limit its application to wood imported prior to 2008 and composite wood products, and would allow an innocent owner defense to forfeiture actions. A different approach is taken by S. 2062, which would eliminate any reference to violations of foreign laws and end criminal prosecutions for violating the act.

BACKGROUND

The Lacey Act addresses conservation by targeting trade. As adopted in 1900, the Lacey Act made it a federal crime to ship game killed in violation of one state's laws to another state.[1] It also regulated the introduction of non-native species and prohibited shipment of wildlife without clear identification of the contents and shipper.[2] This report will examine the portions of the Lacey Act that pertain to transporting fish, wildlife, and plants that were taken in violation of another law, and will not address the other provisions of the act.

While it has been amended many times since 1900, the Lacey Act's format has remained the same: with respect to fish, wildlife, and plants, generally speaking, it is a violation of the act to violate another law, be it state, federal, tribal, or foreign. Accordingly, making a case under the Lacey Act requires a violation of an underlying law as well as a violation of the act itself.

The act has a broad reach. It applies to any person, with *person* defined to include individuals, corporations, government officials, and government agencies.[3] It covers violations of state, federal, tribal, or foreign laws (including regulations) that regulate "the taking, possession, importation, exportation, transportation, or sale" of wildlife or plants.[4] It is enforced by the Fish and Wildlife Service (FWS) of the Department of the Interior, the National Oceanic and Atmospheric Administration of the Department of Commerce, Customs and Border Protection (CBP) of the Department of

Homeland Security, and the Animal and Plant Health Inspection Service (APHIS) and the Forest Service of the Department of Agriculture.[5]

The 2008 Amendments

In 2008, the Lacey Act was amended, expanding the definition of plants to include trees and plant products, and prohibiting different types of trade related to plants. In August 2011, FWS executed search warrants for the premises of Gibson Guitar Corp. reportedly based on Gibson's violations of the 2008 Amendments when Gibson allegedly imported unfinished wood in violation of India's export laws. Because Gibson has claimed its imported wood was sustainably harvested, some argue that the 2008 Amendments do not conserve environmental resources exclusively but can hurt US workers by enforcing foreign laws that protect foreign workers. Others argue that the act protects US jobs.

Legislative History of the 2008 Amendments

According to the legislative history for the 2008 amendments, its purposes were two-fold: to promote ecosystem protection and to aid the US timber industry. According to the House Conference Report, the amendments address the following problems:

> [I]llegal logging undermines responsible forest enterprises by distorting timber markets with unfair competition and price undercutting. Illegal logging also threatens the conservation of forest resources, wildlife, and biodiversity, by facilitating forest conversion to non-forest uses and depleting or completely eliminating certain forest ecosystems or the habitat of certain forest dependent wildlife. Finally, illegal logging results in a loss of revenue when taxes or royalties are not paid that could otherwise be invested in sustainable forest management or economic development.[6]

Senator Wyden, a co-sponsor of a bill that led to the 2008 Amendments described the benefits of the act as follows: "This legislation will raise the risks for illegal trade without harming legal trade and will be an important step toward leveling a playing field currently stacked against the US forest products industry and importers and retailers committed to trading in legal wood products."[7]

Senator Alexander, another co-sponsor, discussed the bill's projected economic impact of illegal timber imports: "[I]t is an estimated $1 billion a year in depressed prices and reduced exports. It depresses prices $500 million to $700 million annually. It means the people who play by the rules in the United States are having money taken from them by criminals who don't play by the rules in other countries ..."[8]

PROHIBITIONS RELATED TO WILDLIFE

Because of the complexity of the act, involving federal, state, and/or foreign laws, the act is best analyzed with respect to the type of goods it seeks to protect. This report will first look at those parts of the Lacey Act pertaining to wildlife. Plants will be discussed later in the context of the 2008 Amendments. However, as will be discussed in greater detail below, with respect to both wildlife and plants, penalties for Lacey Act violations are based on the degree of knowledge or care taken by the alleged offender, while forfeiture of protected wildlife and plants under the Lacey Act is on a strict liability basis.

Violations of US or Tribal Law

The act uses the term *fish or wildlife* to include "any wild animal, whether living or dead ... [including] any part, product, egg, or offspring thereof."[9] This report will simply use the term *wildlife*. There are two types of prohibited acts pertaining to wildlife. The first makes it illegal to "import, export, transport, sell, receive, acquire, or purchase" wildlife if that creature was "taken, possessed, transported, or sold in violation of any law ... of the United States or in violation of any Indian tribal law."[10]

Example[11] 1 (Section 3372(a)(1))

Assume a person has killed a hummingbird in the state of Oklahoma. That is a violation of the Migratory Bird Treaty Act (MBTA), a federal law.[12] However, it is not a violation of the Lacey Act. Even though wildlife was taken in violation of a federal law, that wildlife was not then imported, exported, transported, sold, received, acquired, or purchased, as required for a Lacey Act violation.

In this case, a violation of a federal law that regulates wildlife is also a violation of the Lacey Act if the wildlife in question was imported, exported, transported, sold, or received.

Example 2 (Section 3372(a)(1))

Assume a person has killed a hummingbird in the state of Oklahoma. That person has violated the MBTA. That person then sells the feathers to a person in Oklahoma. By making the sale, that person has also violated the Lacey Act because there was a sale of wildlife (which by definition includes parts of that animal) that was taken in violation of a federal law. The buyer also has violated the Lacey Act because the buyer purchased wildlife that was taken in violation of a federal law.

Violations of State or Foreign Law

The second type of wildlife prohibition under the Lacey Act involves interstate or foreign commerce. Section 3372(a)(2)(A) of the Lacey Act makes it illegal to "import, export, transport, sell, receive, acquire, or purchase in interstate or foreign commerce" wildlife if that wildlife was "taken, possessed, transported, or sold in violation of any law or regulation of any State or in violation of any foreign law."[13] For this type of violation, the underlying law must be state or foreign. While the language clearly includes state regulatory violations as a predicate act to a Lacey Act violation ("in violation of any law or regulation of any State"), it is not so clear from the statute whether violations of foreign regulations may also be the basis for a Lacey Act violation. Courts, however, have held that foreign regulations may be the foundation for a charge.

The Eleventh Circuit reviewed congressional intent before holding that violations of foreign regulations and other legally binding provisions are also a basis for making a Lacey Act enforcement case.[14]

Example 3 (Section 3372(a)(2)(A))

Assume a person has killed a deer in violation of Wisconsin's hunting laws. The deer is field dressed and consumed without leaving the state or entering commerce. There is no violation of the Lacey Act because there is no interstate commerce.

The Ninth Circuit found that Congress used the term "foreign law" so it would encompass the many forms that foreign legal edicts may take.[15]

Example 4 (Section 3372(a)(2)(A))

Assume a person has killed a deer in violation of Wisconsin's hunting laws by hunting in an area where it is not allowed, for example, a petting zoo. The venison is sold to a person in interstate commerce. Because interstate commerce was involved, the seller has violated the Lacey Act. Likewise, the buyer also has violated the Lacey Act.

The Lacey Act has an expanded use of the term *sale* in the context of wildlife violations. It deems an offer to provide guiding or outfitting services, or to provide a hunting or fishing license or permit as a sale.[16] Accordingly, obtaining a hunting license in violation of tribal law can be the predicate violation of the Lacey Act.[17]

Before a violation occurs under either Section 3372(a)(1) or Section 3372(a)(2)(A), both parts of the Lacey Act must be triggered—the underlying or predicate law and then the Lacey Act. Courts must determine the validity of both the predicate violation and the action that triggers the Lacey Act charge. Where the predicate violation is one of foreign law or regulation, the federal courts have the authority to determine whether a foreign law has been violated.[18] Federal courts also have jurisdiction when the underlying violation is one of tribal law.[19]

Establishing violations of foreign law can lead to complicated situations. For example, the United States seized the hide and horns of an Afghan Urial, a type of big horn sheep, imported to Virginia from Pakistan. The importer of the animal argued that Pakistan had no national law protecting the Urial and that he had a valid permit from the province where it was taken. The Fifth Circuit held that a Pakistani law that prohibited the export of wild animal hides barred the export of the Urial pelt.[20] In another case a man was convicted of importing spiny lobsters to the United States that were caught in violation of Honduras law. By the time the conviction was appealed, "the Honduran government reversed its position; it [refuted] the validity of the laws it previously verified."[21] The Eleventh Circuit held that Honduras law at the time the conduct occurred prohibited harvesting the spiny lobsters and upheld the Lacey Act conviction.[22]

In determining that the predicate violation occurred, the court does not have to find that the procedures of that jurisdiction were followed. Federal procedural rules apply.[23] For example, the Fourth Circuit has held that the general federal statute of limitations applies.[24] For a Lacey Act violation, there is a five-year statute of limitations.[25]

PROHIBITIONS RELATED TO PLANTS

The Lacey Act definition of plant was expanded in 2008 to include any wild member of the plant kingdom including roots, seeds, parts, or products, including trees.[26] Prior to the 2008 Amendments, the Lacey Act applied only to those plants that were indigenous to the United States and listed under one of the following: the Endangered Species Act (ESA); the Convention on International Trade in Endangered Species of Wild Fauna and Flora (CITES); or a state law to conserve species threatened with extinction.[27] It did not expressly apply to plant products. The revised definition has some exclusions, such as for scientific research and for plants that will be transplanted.[28] The Lacey Act prohibits four types of acts related to plants and requires submission of a declaration for importing plants.

Violations of US or Tribal Law

One prohibited activity is identical for plant violations as it is for wildlife violations. The Lacey Act makes it illegal to "import, export, transport, sell, receive, acquire, or purchase" plants if the plant was "taken, possessed, transported, or sold in violation of [US or Indian tribal law]."[29] As for the wildlife violations, these cases tend to be fact-specific. For example, the saguaro cactus, an icon of the American Southwest, is not protected under federal law but is under Arizona State law. Accordingly, taking a saguaro cactus would not be a Lacey Act violation under Section 3372(a)(1),[30] but would be under Section 3372(a)(2)(B), as discussed below.

Example 5 (Section 3372(a)(1))

A person in New York found sandplain gerardia on federal lands, a plant listed as endangered under the ESA. That person kills the plant. The person has violated the ESA,[31] but has not violated the Lacey Act because there has been no act of import, export, transport, sale, receipt, acquisition, or purchase of the plant.

Example 6 (Section 3372(a)(1))

A person digs up a Kuenzler hedgehog cactus (an endangered species) from a state park, which violates state law, and sells it to someone in another state. The buyer plants it in the perfect spot and it flourishes. Even though the plant does not die, there is still a violation of the ESA, which prohibits digging up endangered plants in violation of state law, as well as buying or selling them in interstate commerce.[32] Therefore, both the seller and the buyer have violated the ESA. Because there was a sale, both have also violated the Lacey Act.

Violations of State or Foreign Law Protecting Plants

The 2008 Amendments added three other prohibited acts related to plants. The first directly relates to laws that conserve plants. It prohibits importing, exporting, transporting, selling, receiving, acquiring, or purchasing any plant in interstate or foreign commerce if that plant was taken, possessed, transported, or sold in violation of state or foreign laws that

1. protect plants;
2. regulate the theft of plants;
3. regulate the taking of plants from a park, forest reserve, or other officially protected area;
4. regulate the taking of plants from an officially designated area; or
5. regulate the taking of plants without, or contrary to, required authorization.[33]

Under this section, Section 3372(a)(2)(B)(i), it is illegal to take a plant, including a tree or a plant product, in interstate commerce, if the state or foreign country protected the specific plant in some way or protected the area from which the plant was taken, and that protection was violated.

Example 7 (Section 3372(a)(2)(B)(i))

A person takes wild sage leaves from the roadside of Turkey, and then brings the leaves into the United States for the person's own use. Assume it is against Turkish law to pick sage leaves off roadside plants without authorization. A Lacey Act violation occurred because the person imported sage leaves that violated a foreign law.

Under the 2008 Amendments, taking a saguaro cactus, as discussed above, would be prosecuted under Section 3372(a)(2)(B).

Example 8 (Section 3372(a)(2)(B)(i))

A person picks leaves of a plant that grows only in Turkey from the roadside and then brings the leaves into the United States to sell. Assume this violates Turkish law. Assume it is against US law to sell those leaves. Prior to enactment of the 2008 Amendments there would be no Lacey Act violation, as the definition of *plant* at the time required that the plant be indigenous to the United States (or listed under ESA, CITES, or state law) for the prohibitions to apply, and underlying foreign law was not applicable in the pre-2008 Lacey Act.

Violations of State or Foreign Law Requiring Fees

The other two plant prohibitions are less directly linked to conservation. One prohibition under the 2008 Amendments makes it illegal to import, export, transport, sell, receive, acquire, or purchase a plant in interstate or foreign commerce that was "taken, possessed, transported, or sold without the payment of appropriate royalties, taxes, or stumpage fees required for the plant by any law or regulation of any State or any foreign law."[34] Under this provision, the type of plant or the location of the plant is not at issue. The predicate act is based on whether the plant was harvested legally in relation to required fees.

Prohibiting import, export, sales, and purchases of timber based on payment of fees could be argued as having a conservation interest by limiting illegally harvested trees, even if the illegality is related to paying fees, rather than the type or locale of the trees. The theory that this prohibition supports conservation is that lawless harvesting limits the economic advantage timber harvesting typically brings, such as funds for reforestation or other protections.[35]

From an enforcement perspective, these violations can be easier to prove because there will be paperwork showing whether the fees were paid (as opposed to proof of illegal origin, for example), and the conservation benefits can more easily be realized.

Example 9 (Section 3372(a)(2)(B)(ii))

An American furniture manufacturer imports oak from Canada knowing that the price is good because the timber company selling the wood "knows a guy" who can avoid paying fees for cutting the trees. The American furniture company has violated the Lacey Act even though it was the timber company or "the guy" that did not pay the fees. The act prohibits purchase of timber taken or sold without paying appropriate taxes and royalties. It does not have to be the purchaser or importer that was required to pay the fees.

Violations of State or Foreign Law Restricting Export

The last prohibition added by the 2008 Amendments makes it illegal to import, export, transport, sell, receive, acquire, or purchase a plant in interstate or foreign commerce that was "taken, possessed, transported, or sold in violation of any limitation under any law or regulation of any State, or under any foreign law, governing the export or transshipment of plants."[36]

Because there is no specific requirement that the export law relate to conservation, some could contend this provision is more likely to preserve trade advantages, rather than to protect ecosystems. But the argument could be made that any restriction of trade in wood and wood products provides conservation benefit by potentially limiting the amount of wood that is harvested and exported.

These export laws can serve as an enforcement "choke point" for that jurisdiction. Local officials can moderate how the wood being processed was taken, thus serving a conservation purpose. For example, by reviewing wood finishing, the foreign government has the opportunity to review harvesting issues, such as location and types of wood. Another conservation benefit to enforcing foreign export laws can be illustrated by the example of a country with a limited supply of a type of wood but an unlimited demand for that wood worldwide.

If processing were allowed to occur outside of the country, that rare timber would be harvested without any limitation. By requiring local processing, harvest is limited to the speed of domestic manufacturing, thus conserving the timber.

These provisions may also aid US timber industry interests by restricting imported wood and wood products.

Example 10 (Section 3372(a)(2)(B)(iii))

Under the law of a foreign country, only hand-made toothpicks may be exported. That same country has no restrictions on harvesting a common tree. A US importer imports machine-made toothpicks, made of that common tree. The importer has violated the Lacey Act because it has imported plants (or plant products) in violation of a foreign law governing export of plants.

Declaration

The 2008 Amendments also added a requirement for a declaration to be prepared by those importing plants under the act. Under Section 3372(f), after a period of time following enactment of the amendments (which occurred May 22, 2008), it became illegal to import a plant (or plant product) without a declaration showing the following:

- the scientific name (including genus and species);
- the value;
- the quantity, including unit of measure; and
- the country from which the plant was taken.[37]

The declaration is submitted by the importer at the time of import. A copy of the form is maintained in either electronic or paper form by APHIS and CBP.

The 2008 Amendments required the declaration as of December 15, 2008. However, in response to concerns about the complexity of implementing the declaration requirement, especially for importers of wood products, APHIS established a delayed enforcement schedule, setting compliance stages for some more complicated products for April 1, 2010.[38] Certain products, such as wooden furniture, still are not on an enforcement schedule. (See the *Appendix* for the Schedule.) While the declarations were required for all products as of December 15, 2008, APHIS said it would not prosecute for failure to have a declaration until the dates indicated in the implementation schedule.[39]

The 2008 Amendments also required APHIS to evaluate the declaration process within two years of enactment.[40] In February 2011, APHIS published a notice that it was initiating its review and seeking comments on the implementation of declarations.[41] A report must be submitted to Congress within six months of completing the review.[42]

PENALTIES: CIVIL VIOLATIONS, FELONIES, MISDEMEANORS, AND FORFEITURE

While Section 3372 states what actions are not legal, Section 3373 tells what actions may be punished. The Lacey Act provides for civil and criminal penalties as well as forfeiture of the protected item. Some conduct can be subject to either civil or criminal charges.

The choice is left to the prosecutors at the Department of Justice. These provisions took shape when the Lacey Act was significantly amended in 1981.[43]

Civil Violations

For the violations described in the examples above (as opposed to marking or labeling violations) the standard for a civil violation is whether the person engaged in that conduct "in the exercise of due care should know that the fish or wildlife or plants were taken, possessed, transported, or sold in violation of, or in a manner unlawful under, any underlying law, treaty, or regulation."[44] If so, that person may be assessed "a civil penalty by the Secretary of not more than $10,000 for each such violation."[45]

The penalty is reduced if the value of the wildlife or plants is less than $350.[46] The *exercise of due care* is a common legal phrase meaning the amount of attention a reasonable person in the same circumstances would use. Under this standard, a first-time buyer of imported animals, for example, is likely to be found to have less responsibility than an importer of those animals. It does not excuse deliberate ignorance. Due care requires what is reasonable, such as asking questions. The Senate Report supporting the 1981 Amendments described the standard as follows: " Due care simply requires that a person facing a particular set of circumstances undertake[s] certain steps which a reasonable man would take to do his best to insure that he is not violating the law."[47]

According to that Senate Report, the due care requirement was added to avoid overzealous prosecution of unknowing violators: "The civil penalty provisions are included with the understanding that they will not be administered to penalize innocent purchasers or consumers, but rather with the clear intent that they will be applied fairly in an equitable and nonabusive manner."[48]

Misdemeanors

Similarly, the Lacey Act makes it a criminal misdemeanor for someone "who knowingly engages in conduct prohibited by any provision of this chapter,"[49] and "in the exercise of due care should know that the fish or wildlife or plants were taken, possessed, transported, or sold in violation of, or in a manner unlawful under, any underlying law, treaty or regulation."[50] The criminal misdemeanor provision explicitly requires that the action that triggers the Lacey Act violation be *knowingly* done. This means that the person must know he (or she) is doing the action, such as transporting the item or buying a wildlife or plant product, not that he knows he is doing something wrong.

For the predicate act, the standard for a misdemeanor, like the civil provision, is based on a *due care* standard: it applies to those who "in the exercise of due care should know" that something illegal was occurring. According to that same 1981 Senate Report, this provision was included to avoid leaving "too much potential for abuse and indiscriminate enforcement efforts."[51]

Returning to *Example Two*, above, for illustration, proving the Lacey Act portion of the illegal feather purchase would require the buyer to know only that he was buying a wildlife or plant product, not that he knew he was buying illegal hummingbird feathers. But the predicate violation must also be proved—a court must find that the buyer in the exercise of due care should know that the product was somehow illegal.

Example 2A—Expanded to Consider Misdemeanor Culpability

A person buys a bag of feathers that includes some hummingbird feathers mixed in with legal goose down. It was the same price as every other bag of down. The person knowingly bought feathers, but in the exercise of due care he would have no knowledge that the feathers he bought were illegal. It is unlikely that a court would find the person by exercising due care should have known he was buying feathers that were taken in violation of federal law.

A misdemeanor may be punished by up to one year in jail, in addition to or instead of the fine.

Despite the Lacey Act authorizing a maximum $10,000 fine for the misdemeanor, under the Criminal Fines Improvement Act, the maximum criminal penalty is adjusted to $100,000 for an individual, and $200,000 for an organization.[52]

Example 2B—Expanded to Consider Misdemeanor Culpability

A person buys three tiny green feathers for the same price as a whole bag of down. This person also knowingly committed the act that triggers the Lacey Act by buying the feathers. It is likely that a court would find that this person when buying those tiny feathers did not exercise due care to discover whether a law had been violated. Two factors a court might expect a reasonable person to consider under the circumstances are that the feathers were unusual and that they were more expensive. The failure to ask reasonable questions could support a finding that the second buyer engaged in conduct prohibited by the act (buying feathers) and that any due care would have revealed that the feathers were taken in violation of law, establishing a Lacey Act violation.

Felonies

The felony provision has a higher standard of culpability. Like the misdemeanor provision, it also requires the actor to know he or she was committing the action that triggers the Lacey Act violation—importing, exporting, engaging in the conduct to sell or purchase or attempt to sell or purchase an item taken in violation of another law—but it also requires that the actor know "that the fish or wildlife or plants were taken, possessed, transported, or sold in violation of, or in a manner unlawful under, any underlying law, treaty or regulation."[53] To be a felony there must be knowledge and one of two things: import or export;[54] or commercial conduct and a value of over $350.[55]

These requirements were included to avoid imposing big penalties on smaller offenders, according to the 1981 Senate Report.[56] Additionally, that report indicates congressional intent to allow innocent violators to escape criminal prosecution, "the act's criminal culpability requirement assures that innocent violators of the act will not be subject to criminal penalties."[57] Punishment for committing a felony includes incarceration of no more than five years, a fine of $250,000 for individuals and $500,000 for organizations, or both.[58]

To illustrate the felony provisions, consider *Example 4*, above, in which an Illinois buyer purchased a deer killed in violation of Wisconsin law.

The court must find the buyer knew two elements: (1) that he was buying something; and (2) that the venison he was buying was illegal in some way.

Example 4A—Expanded to Consider Felony Culpability

The buyer purchased the venison at a farmers' market in November (a time when most, if not all states, allow deer hunting). He paid the going rate for the meat. Under this example, a court likely would find that the buyer had not criminally violated the Lacey Act. Everything was consistent with a bona fide purchase. A reasonable person would not know in these circumstances that the venison was tainted, nor in the exercise of due care would discover the underlying violation of law.

Example 4B—Expanded to Consider Felony Liability

The buyer, an avid deer hunter, purchased the fresh venison at midnight in the parking lot of a petting zoo where remains of the deer could be seen in a pile. The price was very cheap and the seller was wearing a mask. It seems likely a court would find the buyer had criminally violated the Lacey Act. The circumstances of the sale/purchase would cause a reasonable person to know something was wrong.

Forfeiture

The Lacey Act also authorizes forfeiture of the illegal items. Forfeiture is where the government confiscates an item involved in a crime.[59] As the Ninth Circuit found in *United States v. 144,744 Pounds of Blue King Crab,* under the law, the illegally taken or imported item is considered contraband, even if possessing it would not otherwise be illegal.[60] If the forfeiture action is civil, the court does not have to find a person liable for wrongdoing. For example, in the case discussed earlier of the Urial (the big horn sheep from Pakistan), the suit was not against the importer for violating the Lacey Act, but was a case where the government seized the hide and horns from the importer.[61] The prosecution was against the contraband itself. Cases in which civil forfeiture is the only issue have case names where the item is named as the defendant. For criminal forfeiture actions, a successful suit requires conviction of the person who owned the contraband.

Forfeiture can serve two purposes: remedial or punitive. According to the Supreme Court, the remedial purposes include preventing forbidden merchandise from circulating, and reimbursing the government for investigation and enforcement expenses.[62] The punitive goals of forfeiture apply to criminal proceedings.

The Lacey Act applies civil forfeiture proceedings to "all fish or wildlife or plants imported, exported, transported, sold, received, acquired, or purchased contrary to [Section 3372 of the act] ... notwithstanding any culpability requirements for civil penalty assessment or criminal prosecution [under Section 3373 of the act]."[63] In situations where the wildlife or plants were part of a "criminal violation of this Act for which a felony conviction is obtained," the act allows civil forfeiture of the "vessels, vehicles, aircraft, and other equipment" used in committing the crime.[64]

Prior to the 2008 Amendments, courts held that there was no innocent owner defense to forfeiture under the Lacey Act. These decisions are based on the act's language that that "*all* fish or wildlife or plants [that violate Section 3372] shall be subject to forfeiture ... "[65] According to the 1981 Senate Report, forfeiture was to occur regardless of culpability: "The strict liability forfeiture section of these amendments would allow the protection of various species from harmful illegal trade by withdrawing illegal shipments from the marketplace even when the violation itself is inadvertent."[66]

The only defense described in that report was where the merchandise was without taint and the import ran afoul of the law only in a "minor, technical" manner.[67]

The Fifth Circuit pointed to that legislative background in finding that "the legislative history establishes that the forfeiture statute provides for strict liability, thereby eliminating any 'innocent owner' defense."[68] A federal court in Florida held that the Lacey Act does not provide for an innocent owner defense.[69]

As referenced above, in *United States v.144,744 Pounds of Blue King Crab*, the Ninth Circuit has held that Lacey Act goods are contraband.[70]

The 2008 Amendments added the statement that civil forfeiture was to be "in accordance with the procedure established under [18 USC. §§981-986]."[71] Under this statute, the Civil Asset Forfeiture Reform Act (CAFRA),[72] the government has the burden of proof by a preponderance of evidence.[73] The person owning the forfeited goods may also seek immediate release of the property pending trial.[74]

CAFRA allows a defense to a civil forfeiture for innocent owners, bona fide purchasers, and heirs.[75] However, under CAFRA, the innocent owner defense cannot be used for contraband. The exclusion states: "no person may assert an ownership interest under this subsection in contraband or other property that it is illegal to possess."[76] As discussed above, the Ninth Circuit found that goods taken in violation of the Lacey Act are contraband. Additionally, the 1981 Senate Report described the goods in the same way: "The act provides for forfeiture of the fish, wildlife and plants on a strict liability basis because the merchandise is, in effect, contraband."[77]

A statement in the House Report on the 2008 Amendments further references the *Blue King Crab* decision to note that incorporating CAFRA by reference may not provide a defense to the strict liability forfeiture provisions under the Lacey Act because of the ruling that goods are contraband under the act.[78]

However, it is possible to have the goods returned while the matter is still administrative, before it is referred to court. This is known as remission. Department of the Interior regulations that apply to forfeitures allow the possibility of remission in administrative forfeitures in rare circumstances. When FWS notifies a person that goods are forfeited, that person may file a petition for remission rather than a claim, which would refer the matter to court.

Under 50 C.F.R. §12.24(f), the regulations provide that "If the Solicitor finds the existence of such mitigation circumstances," goods may be remitted. The only published decision available regarding forfeiture of plant products following the 2008 Amendments considered such a petition before rejecting it.[79]

According to that administrative case, the Solicitor considered "whether the facts demonstrate a person's honest and good faith intent to comply with the law, their diligence and efforts to comply, and whether the facts tend to show a lack of negligence or moral culpability for whatever failure or mistake is involved in the non-compliance ... "[80] This administrative forfeiture process appears consistent with the legislative discussion of allowing release of untainted goods related to innocent trade violations.

Example 11—Forfeiture of Contraband

While visiting Nicaragua, a couple buys a table made of a rare wood protected under US law.

When they enter the United States they lie on the customs declaration, saying the table was a different, non-protected species. They have violated the Lacey Act under Section 3372(a)(1), by transporting an item in violation of United States law by lying on a customs declaration. In addition to any civil or criminal prosecution against the couple, the table is contraband and may be seized by the government.

GIBSON GUITARS AND THE 2008 AMENDMENTS

In August 2011, FWS executed search warrants at Gibson Guitar Corp. premises and seized wood imported from India. Reportedly, the FWS agents were armed. It does not appear any arrests were made at the time. According to a statement from Gibson, the wood was certified by the Forest Stewardship Council[81] as sustainably harvested and was seized by FWS because it was "not finished by Indian workers."[82] FWS and the Department of Justice (DOJ) are not commenting on the case.

Section 3375(b) of the Lacey Act authorizes federal agents to carry firearms when enforcing the act. It also allows execution of search and arrest warrants, including searching any vessels, packages, containers, documents, or permits related to the action.

Background

To make sense of the statements in the affidavit prepared to obtain the search warrants, it helps to have some background of relevant trade terminology. Countries generally use the International Harmonized Commodity Description and Coding System (HS) to identify items being shipped. The United States implements the HS in the Harmonized Tariff Schedule of the United States (HTS). Therefore, where the shipment is of foreign origin, it will be identified with HS. Whether HS or HTS, the numbers correlate to the same items. The APHIS chart in the Appendix uses HTS numbers to identify what wood products required a declaration by what date.

For the purposes of the Gibson investigation, two HS codes are relevant. The first is HS 4407— wood split lengthwise that is greater than 6 mm thick. The second is HS 4408—wood veneers, less than 6 mm thick. According to a US customs ruling in 1993, fingerboards for musical instruments, such as guitars and violins, are covered under HS 4407, meaning they are greater than 6 mm thick.[83] Veneer is defined by *Webster's New Collegiate Dictionary* as "a thin sheet of a material: a layer of wood of superior value or excellent grain to be glued to an inferior wood."

According to the affidavit prepared to obtain the Gibson search warrants, "India prohibits the export of products classified under HS Code 4407 for all plant species harvested in India, without exception."[84] Therefore, any wood exported from India under HS 4407 violates Indian law. The affidavit also indicates that exporting wood veneers from India under HS 4408 is legal.[85]

What the Affidavit for the Gibson Warrants States

In order to obtain the search warrants, a Special Agent of FWS completed an affidavit outlining the basis for the search. Four search warrants were ultimately obtained to search Gibson's manufacturing, rough mill, and corporate locations, as well as to search a delivery service. Two shipments formed the basis for the Affidavit: a shipment of ebony from India on June 27, 2011; and a shipment of rosewood and ebony from India on June 20, 2011, which was investigated after the June 27 shipment.[86]

June 27, 2011, Shipment

According to the Affidavit, a CPB official at the Dallas airport suspected a June 27, 2011, shipment of Indian ebony violated the Lacey Act and referred the shipment to an FWS inspector.[87] The FWS inspector, CBP officer, and the APHIS specialist physically identified the shipment as containing sawn Indian ebony of a thickness of 10 mm described under HS 4407.[88] Multiple pieces of documentation accompanied this shipment. (See *Table 1*.) The information on the documents was not consistent, identifying different HS codes (for veneer, for fingerboards, for completed musical instrument parts); and different importers (one in Germany, one in Canada, and Gibson).

The only form that identified the contents as being under HS 4407 and the ultimate receiver being Gibson, according to the information in the Affidavit, was the Lacey Act declaration submitted by Gibson. The declaration was submitted after the investigation had started. That declaration indicated that the shipment for Gibson contained ebony fingerboards under HS 4407. The problem is that India prohibits export of wood under HS 4407, according to the Affidavit. If the Gibson declaration is true, India export law has been violated. If India export law has been violated, it is possible that the predicate violation of the Lacey Act has been triggered and that a violation of Section 3372(a)(2)(B)(iii) has occurred. As discussed above, that section states that a Lacey Act violation has occurred if an item has been imported, exported, transported, sold, received, acquired, or purchased in interstate or foreign commerce and that item was taken, possessed, transported, or sold in violation of a state or foreign law that governs the export or transshipment of plants. There are no statements in the Affidavit regarding an Indian law protecting ebony or requiring royalties or fees, and thus it appears that FWS is not making a case that there is a violation of either Section 3372(a)(2)(B)(i)—pertaining to foreign laws protecting plants; or Section 3372(a)(2)(B)(ii)—

pertaining to foreign laws requiring payment of royalties, taxes, or stumpage fees.

Any certification by the Forest Stewardship Council of the timber product would seem irrelevant, as forestry practices do not appear to be the issue in this case.

Table 1. Documentation Accompanying June 27, 2011, Shipment

Document	Contents as Declared on Form	HS Number	Ultimate Receiver of Goods	Other Information
Air Way Bill 589 2025 5804			Theodor Nagel, Gmbh (of Germany	Contact Luthier Mercantile upon import. Marked for direct transport to Nashville, TN
Customs and Border Protection Form 3461 (US Customs entry declaration)	Veneer Sheets less than 6 mm	HS 4408.90.0195	Luthier Mercantile (of Canada)	
Indian export declaration (June 10, 2011)	Indian ebony	HS 9209.92.00 (finished parts of musical instruments)		
Certificate of Origin from India	Indian ebony finger boards, 10 mm thick		Nashville Airport	
Lacey Act Declaration (USDA Form PPQ) (June 17, 2011)	Ebony fingerboards for guitars: *Diospyros ebenum,* harvested in India.	HS 4407.99.96	Gibson Guitar Corp.	Document submitted after shipment was referred to FWS for investigation on June 27, 2011

Source: Congressional Research Service, based on information from John M. Rayfield, FWS, Affidavit in Support of Search Warrant # 11-MJ-1067 A, B, C, D, pp. 9-11 (August 18, 2011).

Note: Blanks in the Table indicate that information was not available, but do not suggest that information was required.

June 20, 2011, Shipment

The Affidavit also recounts facts relating to an earlier shipment that was discovered after the June 27, 2011, shipment. Again, CPB alerted FWS to a possible Lacey Act violation, in this case Indian rosewood and Indian ebony imported on June 20, 2011.[89] The details about this shipment's documentation are not as clear as for the June 27 shipment. However, the Affidavit indicates that the US customs import declaration identifies Luthier Mercantile as the ultimate receiver of the goods, but that an email from Luthier Mercantile identified Gibson Guitar as the importer.[90] The Affidavit indicates that the shipment was "sawn Indian ebony and sawn Indian rosewood imported under HS code 4407."[91]

While Indian rosewood does not appear to be a protected species under CITES or the ESA, other types of rosewood do have import limitations. CITES lists Brazilian rosewood (*Dalbergia nigra*), Honduran rosewood (*Dalbergia stevensonii*), and Nicaraguan rosewood (*Dalbergia retusa*), thus restricting their trade. No similar restrictions of ebony were found.

Other Shipments to Gibson

The Affidavit indicates that prior to these two shipments, Gibson has submitted Lacey Act declarations for wood products from India eleven times since August 2010.[92] According to the Affidavit, the CPB database shows eleven shipments of rosewood and/or ebony from India to Gibson under HS 4407.[93]

FWS brought a forfeiture action related to a Gibson import of ebony from Madagascar in 2009.[94] If Gibson is charged under Section 3372(a)(B)(iii) for any of these shipments, rather than DOJ proceeding with a civil forfeiture action only,[95]

DOJ would need to show that Gibson *knew* that the shipment violated a law related to export.

It would not have to show that Gibson knew the specific Indian law, only that it was doing something illegal.[96] According to the Ninth Circuit, the Lacey Act does not require "that the violator know all the details of the statutes and regulations that make the conduct unlawful. It suffices that he knows, not only that he is importing or exporting [the plant or animal], but also that the [plants or animals] are tainted by a violation of some law."[97] A court may consider Gibson's business importing wood;[98] that it has been charged with an import violation before;[99] and/or that the documentation was inconsistent (perhaps to conceal the violation) as evidence that Gibson knew the import was against the law.

LEGISLATION IN THE 112TH CONGRESS

The 112th Congress is considering legislation to alter the Lacey Act. On October 17, 2011, an amendment was proposed to an agriculture appropriations bill that targeted agency funding:

> None of the funds appropriated or otherwise made available by this title shall be used to pay the salaries and expenses of personnel to enforce the provisions of section 3(a)(2) of the Lacey Act Amendments of 1981 ... with respect to a plant taken, possessed, transported, or sold in violation of a foreign law unless the applicable foreign government has initiated proceedings against the company or individual under the foreign law.100

This would have affected APHIS enforcement had it passed, but would not have restricted FWS or CBP funding, neither of which are under the Department of Agriculture. By requiring foreign enforcement before US enforcement were possible, this amendment would have reversed over a century of Lacey Act precedent.

Two other bills regarding the Lacey Act are pending. H.R. 3210 would limit the application of the 2008 Amendments. It would amend the act to provide statutory protection for plant or plant products assembled or imported prior to the date the 2008 Amendments were enacted.[101] This would serve as what is commonly called a *grandfather clause* for actions prior to May 22, 2008. While the 2008 Amendments did not take effect before that date, the law does not have an effective date for when the predicate action may have occurred. Accordingly, without the provision proposed in H.R. 3210, Section 3, if a musical instrument was sold in 2010 made of wood that was illegally taken in 2002, that sale violates the Lacey Act. APHIS has proposed regulations that would revise the declaration requirement for pre-2008 material.[102]

Additionally, as discussed above, the Lacey Act requires knowledge of or reasonable care to discover the underlying violation, so only those buyers and sellers who knew or should have known of the underlying problem would be subject to prosecution. Additionally, the Director of FWS has stated that the agency is not pursuing enforcement against owners of instruments, but is focusing on importers.[103]

Section 3 of the bill would also assist innocent owners by excluding the CAFRA provision that blocks the innocent owner defense for contraband or goods taken illegally. Innocent owners could also be aided by Section 7, which would authorize a certification program so that plants and plant products could be certified as legal for the purposes of sale and resale.

H.R. 3210 also would limit the types of wood that were covered by the declaration requirement. Section 3 would require a declaration only for wood that was "entered for consumption."

The designation of "entered for consumption"[104] applies to wood products that will be used in commerce once they enter the United States and are not for personal use only. This appears intended to exclude people transporting musical instruments for personal use from the declaration requirements. Section 3 also would change the declaration condition for providing scientific name, the value and quantity, and the country of origin, requiring only solid wood importers to complete that information.

Particle board and medium density fiberboard importers would no longer have to detail where their composite wood came from. To the extent that composite wood is made of spruce, pine, or fir, APHIS has already proposed regulations to limit the declaration requirements.[105]

Section 4 of the bill would cap the civil penalty for a first violation at $250.

Section 5 of the bill would postpone the deadline of the APHIS report on the declaration implementation to 180 days after H.R. 3210 is enacted. The extended deadline would allow consideration of the changes from H.R. 3210. Section 5 would also direct FWS to evaluate the feasibility of providing a database of "laws of foreign countries from which plants are exported." No additional funding for these programs is provided by the bill.

H.R. 3210, Section 8 directs the Federal Trade Commission (FTC) to study the competitiveness of the US market for raw materials that are used for musical instrument manufacture. The FTC report would be due 180 days after enactment.

Senate bill S. 2062 takes a different approach to amending the act. It proposes excising all references to violations of foreign law from the Lacey Act, making actions illegal only if they have run afoul of state, federal, or tribal law. Accordingly, S. 2062 would effectively halt any protections the Lacey Act provided to the domestic timber industry from illegal foreign harvesting.

The bill would also eliminate any criminal prosecutions, including the power to issue warrants and make arrests, while capping civil penalties at $200,000, an amount smaller than the current criminal maximum penalty of $250,000 for individuals and $500,000 for organizations. It would alter the forfeiture proceedings by eliminating the incorporation by reference of customs laws. It does not address the issue of strict liability for forfeitures.

APPENDIX. DECLARATIONS ENFORCEMENT CHART

I December 15, 2008	II April 1, 2009	III October 1, 2009	IV April 1, 2010
PPS Plant Import Declaration Form will be available on Web site, and accepted after December 15, 2008. Domestic and International Outreach.	HTS Chapters: Ch. 44 Headings (wood & articles of wood) 4401—(Fuel wood) 4403—(Wood in the rough) 4404 (Hoopwood; poles, piles, stakes) 4406—(Railway or tramway sleepers) 4407 (Wood sawn or chipped lengthwise) 4409—(Wood continuously shaped) 4417—(Tools, tool handles, broom handles) 4418 (Builders' joinery and carpentry of wood)	HTS Chapters: Ch. 44 Headings (wood & articles of wood) 4402—Wood charcoal 4412—Plywood, veneered panels, except 44129906 and 44129957 4414—Wooden frames 4419 Tableware & kitchenware of wood 4420—Wood marquetry, caskets, statuettes PLUS PHASE II	HTS Chapters: Ch. 44 Headings (wood & articles of wood) 4421—Other articles of wood Ch. 66 Headings (umbrellas, walking sticks, riding crops) 6602 Walking sticks, whips, crops. Ch. 82 Headings (tools, implements) 8201—Hand tools Ch. 92 Headings (musical instruments) 9201—Pianos 9202 Other stringed instruments Ch. 93 Headings (arms and ammunition) 9302—Revolvers and pistols 93051020–Parts and accessories for revolvers and pistols Ch. 94 Headings (furniture, etc.) 940169—Seats with wood frames Ch. 95 Headings (toys, games & sporting equipment) 950420 Articles and accessories for billiards Ch. 97 Headings (works of art) 9703—Sculptures PLUS PHASES II & III

Figure A-1. Phase-In Schedule of Enforcement of the Declaration Requirement for Goods of, or Containing, Plants or Plant Products.

End Notes

[1] Act of May 25, 1900, §3, 31 Stat. 187.

[2] Act of May 25, 1900, §2 and §4, respectively, 31 Stat. 188.

[3] 16 USC. §3371(e).

[4] 16 USC. §3371(d).

[5] See, 16 USC. §3371(h) (defining Secretary as the Secretary of the Interior and the Secretary of Agriculture); 16 USC. §3373(a) (stating that the provisions will be enforced by "the Secretary, the Secretary of Transportation, or the Secretary of the Treasury").

[6] H.Rept. 110-627; 1981 USCCAN p. 127, 536. (May 13, 2008).

[7] S. Cong. Rec. 15622, at 15635 (December 14, 2007).

[8] S. Cong. Rec. at 13968 (November 6, 2007).

[9] 16 USC. §3371(a).

[10] 16 USC. §3372(a)(1).

[11] The Examples in this report should be considered hypothetical situations and not factually or legally true.

[12] 16 USC. §703(a).

[13] 16 USC. §3372(a)(2)(A).

[14] See United States v. McNab, 331 F.3d 1228 (11th Cir. 2003).

[15] United States v. 594,464 Pounds of Salmon, 871 F.2d 824, 826 (9th Cir.1989).

[16] 16 USC. §3372(c).

[17] See United States v. March, 111 Fed. Appx. 888 (9th Cir. 2004).

[18] Fed. R. Civ. P. 44.1: "... In determining foreign law, the court may consider any relevant material or source, including testimony, whether or not submitted by a party or admissible under the Federal Rules of Evidence. The court's determination must be treated as a ruling on a question of law."

[19] United States v. March, 111 Fed. Appx. 888 (9th Cir. 2004).

[20] United States v. One Afghan Urial Ovis Orientalis Blanfordi Fully Mounted Sheep, 964 F.2d 474 (5th Cir. 1992).

[21] United States v. McNab, 331 F.3d 1228, 1232 (11th Cir. 2003).

[22] United States v. McNab, 331 F.3d 1228, 1242 (11th Cir. 2003).

[23] See United States v. Thomas, 887 F.2d 1341, 1348-49 (9th Cir. 1989) (holding that the federal five-year statute of limitations applied, not the state one-year statute of limitations).

[24] United States v. Borden, 10 F.3d 1058, 1062 (4th Cir. 1993) (rejecting the argument that the state one-year statute of limitations applied).

[25] 18 USC. §3282(a). See Agency Holding Corp. v. Malley-Duff & Assocs., Inc., 483 US 143, 155 (1987) (holding in a RICO case that "if no statute specifically defines a limitations period ... for a particular offense, a 'catchall' statute operates to forbid prosecution, trial, or punishment 'unless the indictment is found or the information is instituted within five years next after such offense shall have been committed'").

[26] 16 USC. §3371(f).

[27] Prior to enactment of the 2008 Amendments, the act defined plant as: "any wild member of the plant kingdom, including roots, seeds, and other parts thereof (but excluding common food crops and cultivars) which is indigenous to any State and which is either (A) listed on an appendix to the Convention on International Trade in Endangered Species of Wild Fauna and Flora, or (B) listed pursuant to any State law that provides for the conservation of species threatened with extinction." 16 USC. §3371(f) (2007).

[28] The regulatory definitions of common food crops and cultivars have not completed the rulemaking process. A draft definition was issued on August 4, 2010. 75 Fed. Reg. 46859.

[29] 16 USC. §3372(a)(1).

[30] See United States v. Miller, 981 F.2d 439 (9th Cir. 1992) (case pre-dating the 2008 Amendments).

[31] 16 USC. §1538(a)(2).

[32] 16 USC. §1538(a)(2).

[33] 16 USC. §3372(a)(2)(B).

[34] 16 USC. §3372(a)(2)(B)(ii).

[35] See Cong. Rec. E533 (March 13, 2007) (Rep. Blumenauer: "By avoiding export duties, timber royalties and taxes on their profits, companies operating unlawfully are robbing national governments of in excess of $15 billion annually on public lands alone. This loss in revenue decreases governments' ability to invest in the forestry sector to promote sustainable forest management and conserve their natural forest resources").

[36] 16 USC. §3372(a)(2)(B)(iii).

[37] 16 USC. §3372(f)(1).

[38] 74 Fed. Reg. 45415 (September 2, 2009).

[39] 74 Fed. Reg. at 45416 (September 2, 2009).

[40] 16 USC. §3372(f)(4).

[41] 76 Fed. Reg. 10874 (February 28, 2011).

[42] 16 USC. §3372(f)(5).

[43] P.L. 97-79.

[44] 16 USC. §3373(a)(1). Pursuant to Debt Collection Improvement Act of 1996 (P.L. 104-134) this penalty may be increased by the agency by publishing a notice in the Federal Register.

[45] 16 USC. §3373(a)(1).

[46] 16 USC. §3373(a)(1).

[47] S. Rept. 97-123; 1981 USC.C.A.N. 1748, 1757-58.

[48] S. Rept. 97-123; 1981 USC.C.A.N. 1748, 1757.

[49] 16 USC. §3373(d)(2)—but not marking or labeling offenses.

[50] 16 USC. §3373(d)(2).

[51] S. Rept. 97-123; 1981 USC.C.A.N. 1748, 1750.

[52] The Criminal Fines Improvement Act of 1987 enhances criminal fines for those laws whose criminal fines have not been adjusted since 1987. The Criminal Fines Improvement Act applies two steps: first, classification of the offense based on the length of the incarceration provided by the underlying act (18 USC. §3559); and second, calculation of the fine based on the offense classification (18 USC. §3571).

[53] 16 USC. §3373(d)(1).

[54] 16 USC. §3373(d)(1)(A).

[55] 16 USC. §3373(d)(1)(B).

[56] S. Rept. 97-123; 1981 USC.C.A.N. 1748, 1758.

[57] S. Rept. 97-123; 1981 USC.C.A.N. 1748, 1759.

[58] 16 USC. §3373(d)(1). The Lacey Act indicates a maximum fine of $20,000. The fines in the text are based on the enhanced amounts under the Criminal Fines Improvement Act.

[59] For a broader analysis of forfeiture, see CRS Report 97-139, Crime and Forfeiture, by Charles Doyle.

[60] United States v. 144,774 Pounds of Blue King Crab, 410 F.3d 1131 (9th Cir. 2005) (holding that crab taken illegally was property that was illegal to possess and therefore fit the definition of contraband).

[61] United States v. One Afghan Urial Ovis Orientalis Blanfordi Fully Mounted Sheep, 964 F.2d 474 (5th Cir. 1992).

[62] One Lot Emerald Cut Stones v. United States, 409 US 232, 237 (1972).

[63] 16 USC. §3374(a)(1).

[64] 16 USC. §3374(a)(2).

[65] 16 USC. §3374(a)(1) (emphasis added).

[66] S. Rept. 97-123; 1981 USC.C.A.N. 1748, 1760.

[67] S. Rept. 97-123; 1981 USC.C.A.N. 1748, 1760.

[68] United States v. One Afghan Urial Ovis Orientalis Blanfordi Fully Mounted Sheep, 964 F.2d 474, 476 (5th Cir. 1992). See also United States v. 2,507 Live Canary Winged Parakeets, 689 F. Supp. 1106, 1117 (S.D. Fla. 1988).

[69] United States v. Proceeds from Sale of Approximately 15,538 Panulirus Argus Lobster Tails, 834 F. Supp. 385 (S.D. Fla. 1993).

[70] United States v. 144,774 Pounds of Blue King Crab, 410 F.3d 1131 (9th Cir. 2005).

[71] 16 USC. §3374(d).

[72] P.L. 106-185.

[73] 18 USC. §983(c)

[74] 18 USC. §983(f).

[75] 18 USC. §983(d).

[76] 18 USC. §983(d)(4).

[77] S. Rept. 97-123; 1981 USC.C.A.N. 1748, 1760.

[78] H.Rept. 110-882.

[79] US Department of the Interior v. Three Pallets of Tropical Hardwood (Crouch), INV. No. 2009403072, at 3 (Office of the DOI Solicitor June 22, 2010).

[80] US Department of the Interior v. Three Pallets of Tropical Hardwood (Crouch), INV. No. 2009403072, at 4 (Office of the DOI Solicitor June 22, 2010). The Solicitor found no mitigating circumstances "[the importer] did not do all he could within his power to comply with regulations and ensure that the shipment was authorized by an export permit that properly documented the required information." Id. at 6.

[81] The Forest Stewardship Council (FSC) is a non-profit group that reviews forest management and production practices. It describes its certification as providing a basis "for socially and environmentally responsible purchasing decisions." See FSC website, http://www. fsc. org/about-fsc.html.

[82] Gibson Guitar Corp. Responds to Federal Raid (August 25, 2011), available at http://www. gibson.com/en-us/ Lifestyle/News/gibson-0825-2011.

[83] Tariff classification ruling NY 881630 (January 26, 1993) (pertaining to sawn Indian rosewood (Dalbergia latifolia) and sawn Indian ebony (Diospyros ebenum)).

[84] John M. Rayfield, FWS, Affidavit in Support of Search Warrant # 11-MJ-1067 A, B, C, D, p. 4 (August 18, 2011) (hereinafter Affidavit). See also Affidavit, p. 8 ("Further research of ... all other published laws and regulations of the Government of India ... revealed no exceptions to this export prohibition").

[85] Affidavit at 7.

[86] Neither Indian rosewood (Dalbergia latifolia) nor ebony (Diospyros ebenum) appear to be species protected under the Convention on International Trade of Endangered Species of Wild Fauna and Flora (CITES) or other American law.

[87] Affidavit at 8.

[88] Affidavit at 8, 11.

[89] Affidavit at 14 (stating the shipment was discovered on July 28, 2011).

[90] Affidavit at 14.

[91] Affidavit at 14.

[92] Affidavit at 11-12.

[93] Affidavit at 12-13.

[94] United States v. Ebony Wood in Various Forms, No. 3:10-cv-747 (M.D. Tenn. administratively closed September 28, 2011). See Heath E. Combs, Gibson Raid Raises Attention on Lacey Act Enforcement, Furniture Today (September 6, 2011), available at http://www.furnituretoday.com/article/print/542690- Gibson_raid_raises_attention_ on_ Lacey_Act_enforcement.php.

[95] Forfeiture action has been filed. United States v. 25 Bundles of Indian Ebony Wood, No. 3:11-cv-913 (M.D. Tenn. 2011).

[96] See, e.g., United States v. Santillan, 243 F.3d 1125 (9th Cir. 2001) (holding that culpability was demonstrated by the fact that he lied about the parrots he was hiding in his car while crossing into the United States from Mexico).

[97] United States v. Santillan, 243 F.3d 1125, 1129 (9th Cir. 2001).

[98] See United States v. Three Pallets of Tropical Hardwood (Crouch), INV. No. 2009403072, at 5 (Office of the DOI Solicitor June 22, 2010) (rejecting a defense that the declaration requirement was new, holding that "a company that specializes in international shipments should be well versed in the applicable laws that govern such transactions").

[99] See United States v. Kuipers, 49 F.3d 1254 (7th Cir. 1995) (allowing DOJ to introduce other crimes in a Lacey Act case to show defendant knew he was violating the law).

[100] S.Amdt. 765 to H.R. 2112 (112th Congress).

[101] H.R. 3210, §3.
[102] 76 Fed. Reg. 38330 (June 11, 2011).
[103] Daniel Ashe, Director, FWS, at a congressional briefing (September 28, 2011).
[104] 19 C.F.R. §141.0a.
[105] 76 Fed. Reg. 38330 (June 11, 2011).

In: The Lacey Act
Editors: G. E. Morgan and D. Hill

ISBN 978-1-62081-615-8

Chapter 2

THE LACEY ACT: COMPLIANCE ISSUES RELATED TO IMPORTING PLANTS AND PLANT PRODUCTS*

Pervaze A. Sheikh

SUMMARY

The Lacey Act regulates the trade of wildlife and plants and creates penalties for a broad spectrum of violations. In 2008, the Lacey Act was amended to include protections for foreign plants and to require adherence to foreign laws as they pertain to certain conservation and other activities involving plants. Further, the 2008 amendments make it unlawful to submit falsified documents related to any plant or plant product covered by the act, and to import certain plant and plant products without an import declaration.

The primary drivers behind the Lacey Act amendments of 2008 (2008 amendments) were to reduce illegal logging globally and increase the value of US wood exports. Illegal logging is a pervasive problem with economic and environmental consequences. The World Bank estimates that illegal logging costs governments approximately $5 billion annually in lost royalties and an additional $10 billion in lost revenue. Further, if there were no illegally logged wood in the global market, it has been

* This is an edited, reformatted and augmented version of a Congressional Research Service publication, CRS Report for Congress R42119, from www.crs.gov, prepared for Members and Committees of Congress, dated December 12, 2011.

projected that the value of US exports of roundwood, sawnwood, and panels could increase by an average of approximately $460 million each year. A halt to illegal logging would also raise the value of domestic wood production. If this is added to exports, the estimated increase in revenue for companies in the United States could be approximately $1.0 billion annually.

A highly publicized raid on Gibson Guitar Corporation brought to light several existing policy issues related to the 2008 amendments to the Lacey Act. Some issues are broad and address the intent of the act. For example, some question why US importers should be held responsible for violations of foreign law or if the requirements under the Lacey Act actually reduce illegal logging. Other issues are narrow and address certain requirements in the act. For example, several suggest that the declaration requirements for importing plant and plant products are cumbersome and not possible to meet in some cases. Further, some contend that the 2008 amendments should not apply to plants harvested or plant products fabricated before the 2008 amendments were enacted. Countering these arguments are those that reiterate the benefits of the 2008 amendments, primarily reducing illegal logging and increasing the economic value of legally obtained plants and plant products on the market.

Congress is addressing these issues through proposed legislation. H.R. 3210 (The Retailers and Entertainers Lacey Implementation and Enforcement Fairness Act; RELIEF Act) was introduced on October 14, 2011, and addresses issues related to declaration requirements, penalties, reporting requirements, and certification standards, among other things authorized under the Lacey Act. Efforts to address implementation issues are also being pursued through regulations. The Animal and Plant Health Inspection Service (APHIS) is soliciting comments on regulatory options that can address issues related to declaration requirements, and is expected to release a report evaluating the implementation of declaration standards under the 2008 amendments.

INTRODUCTION

The Lacey Act was enacted in 1900 to address game poaching and wildlife laundering, among other things.[1] The Lacey Act regulates the trade of wildlife and plants and creates penalties for a broad spectrum of violations. Violations addressed by the Lacey Act involve domestic and international illegal trade of plants and wildlife. Before the enactment of amendments in 2008, the Lacey Act addressed these issues by making it unlawful for any person[2] to:

- "import, export, transport, sell, receive, acquire, or purchase any fish or wildlife or plant taken, possessed, transported, or sold in violation of any law, treaty, or regulation of the United States or in violation of any Indian tribal law"; and
- "import, export, transport, sell, receive, acquire, or purchase in interstate or foreign commerce any fish or wildlife taken, possessed, transported, or sold in violation of any law or regulation of any state, or in violation of any foreign law;" and any plant taken, possessed, transported, or sold in violation of any state law or regulation.[3]

In 2008, the Lacey Act was amended to include nonindigenous plants and violations of foreign laws pertaining to certain conservation actions and other activities involving plants and plant products.[4] Based in part on these amendments, the Lacey Act now makes it unlawful for any person to import, export, transport, sell, receive, acquire, or purchase in interstate or foreign commerce any plant taken, possessed, transported, or sold in violation of any law or regulation of any state, or any foreign law, that protects plants or that regulates taking or exporting plants and plant products in certain situations.[5] This includes plants taken, possessed, transported, or sold without the payment of appropriate royalties, taxes, or stumpage fees; and plants exported in violation of state or foreign law.

Further, in reference to plants, it is unlawful to import, export, transport, sell, receive, acquire, or purchase any plant or plant product taken, possessed, transported, or sold in violation of any law, treaty, or regulation of the United States or in violation of any Indian tribal law.[6] In addition, the Lacey Act makes it unlawful to falsify or submit falsified documents related to any plant or plant product covered by the act, and to import certain plant and plant products without an import declaration.[7]

The provisions related to fish, wildlife, and plants in reference to laws, treaties, and regulations of the United States and any Indian tribal law were unchanged (although the definition of plants was expanded to include nonindigenous plants).

The 2008 amendments to the Lacey Act (2008 amendments) also expand the definition of a plant to include *any* plants (including foreign plants), whereas before it referred only to plants indigenous to any state or associated commonwealths, territories, or possessions of the United States. A plant is specifically defined as "any wild member of the plant kingdom, including roots, seeds, parts, or products thereof, and including trees from either natural or planted forest stands."[8] There are certain exclusions to this definition of plants, including common cultivars (except trees), common food crops, scientific specimens of plant genetic material to be used for laboratory or field research, and any plant that is to remain planted or be planted or replanted.[9]

The 2008 amendments also require importers of all covered plants and plant products to submit an import declaration to US Customs and Border Protection (CBP) at the time of importation. The law requires that the declaration contain certain information, such as identification of the species and genus of plants or plants used in a product, and country of origin of plants, among other things.[10] The declaration appears to apply to all plant and plant products, including those plants harvested or plant products made before the enactment of 2008 amendments.[11]

The primary drivers behind the 2008 amendments were to reduce illegal logging and to increase the value of US wood exports.[12] International illegal logging is a pervasive problem affecting several countries that produce, export, and import wood and wood products. Some have estimated that between 2% and 4% of softwood lumber[13] and plywood traded globally, and as much as 23% to 30% of hardwood lumber and plywood traded globally, could be from illegal logging activities.[14] Illegal logging is a concern to many because of its economic implications as well as its environmental, social, and political impacts.[15] The World Bank estimates that illegal logging costs governments approximately $5 billion annually in lost royalties and an additional $10 billion in lost revenue.[16] Some are concerned that high US demand for tropical timber from countries in Latin America and Southeast Asia may exacerbate illegal logging. The United States is the world's largest wood products consumer and one of the top importers of tropical hardwoods.[17] For example, the United States is the largest importer of Peruvian mahogany, which some estimate to be 80% illegally logged.[18]

Global illegal logging activities can devalue US exports of timber. Illegally logged wood generally costs less to bring to market than legally logged wood due to nonpayment of fees or taxes, and avoidance of costs related to laws that govern harvesting. This lowers the market price of wood, potentially harming timber operations that operate legally. According to a 2004 report issued by the American Forest and Paper Association, it is estimated that illegal logging of roundwood for wood products depresses world wood prices on average by 7%-16% annually.[19] This affects US producers of wood and their exports. If there were no illegally logged wood in the global market, it has been projected that the value of US exports of roundwood, sawnwood, and panels could increase by an average of approximately $460 million each year.[20] Further, if increases in value for domestic wood production if illegal logging is halted are taken into account, then the increase in value of wood products in the United States each year could be approximately $1.0 billion, according to the study.[21]

The requirements established in the Lacey Act are administered by the Departments of the Interior, Commerce, and Agriculture through their respective agencies. These include the US Fish and Wildlife Service (FWS), National Marine Fisheries Service (NMFS), and Animal and Plant Health Inspection Service (APHIS).

This report summarizes the implementation of the 2008 amendments to the Lacey Act and discusses policy issues related to the amendments. Legislative and regulatory proposals to address these issues are discussed and analyzed.

Gibson Guitar Case

A recent raid of Gibson Guitar Corporation based on alleged Lacey Act violations has brought this law to the attention of Congress. The case illustrates several issues regarding the Lacey Act. On August 24, 2011, federal agents executed four search warrants for Gibson Guitar Corporation facilities in Nashville, TN. The search resulted in the seizure of pallets of wood, electronic files, and guitars. The search warrant affidavit[22] was filed in support of four search warrants and to seize evidence to support potential violations of the Lacey Act under 16 USC. §3372(a)(2)(B) and smuggling laws under 18 USC. §545.[23] The affidavit stated that Gibson Guitar Corporation imported Indian ebony and rosewood in a form that violated Indian law in shipments sent in June 2011.[24] Indian law states that it is unlawful to export products classified under the HS Code 4407 of the International Harmonized Commodity Description and Coding System (HS) for all species of plants harvested in India.[25] Wood under this code is "wood sawn or chipped lengthwise, sliced or peeled, whether or not planed, sanded, or end jointed, or a thickness exceeding 6 mm." For wood to be legally exported from India, it would have to be in a different form (i.e., processed). For example, if the wood had been processed in India into veneer,[26] it could have been classified under HS Code 4408 and been legally exported under Indian law.[27] Further, US Customs issued a tariff clarification ruling on sawn Indian rosewood and ebony imported for the use of manufacturing finger boards for guitars and violins, clarifying that it is illegal to import this wood in this form.[28]

The import of Indian ebony and rosewood classified under HS Code 4407 into the United States appears to be a violation of the Lacey Act under 16 USC. §3372(a)(2)(B)(iii).

This section states that it is unlawful to import in foreign commerce, "any plant taken, possessed, transported, or sold in violation of any limitation under any law or regulation of any State, or under any foreign law, governing the export or transshipment of plants."

The affidavit also notes that Gibson Guitar Corporation has declared shipments of sawn Indian rosewood and ebony from India under HS 4407 eleven times since August 2010.[29] Further, a forfeiture action was brought against Gibson Guitar Corporation regarding a shipment of alleged illegally obtained ebony wood exported from Madagascar to Gibson Guitar Corporation in 2009. Charges have not been filed against Gibson Guitar Corporation in relation to the 2009 and 2011 actions described here.

Summary of Policy Issues Associated with the 2008 Amendments

A recent raid on Gibson Guitar Corporation brought to light several existing policy and legal issues related to the 2008 amendments to the Lacey Act. In broad terms, some question why US importers should be held responsible for violations of foreign law potentially committed by foreign entities (i.e., not US importers). They claim that it is difficult to monitor the harvesting and processing of plants and plant products in foreign countries to make sure that no foreign laws are being violated. Other concerns address specific provisions of the 2008 amendments such as the declaration requirements for plant and plant products imported into the United States. Several businesses have suggested that the declaration requirements for importing plant and plant products are cumbersome and in some cases, not possible to meet.[30] For example, some claim that identifying species for the declaration can be difficult for composite wood materials or some finished products where the wood has been modified from its natural state.[31] Compliance with other requirements in the act is another issue. Some contend that plants and plant products imported before 2008 should be exempt from the law. They note that getting declaration information about these products sometimes years after importation can be difficult.[32] To temper these criticisms of the 2008 amendments of the Lacey Act, some are reiterating the intended positive effects of the amendments, such as the potential economic benefits of reducing illegal logging and the potential environmental benefits of reducing deforestation and corruption associated with the illegal timber trade.[33]

There is congressional interest in this issue in part because of the wide-reaching applicability of the Lacey Act for US industries and consumers and the environmental and economic benefits of reducing illegal logging. The 2008 amendments to the Lacey Act affect all industries that import plant and plant products, including musical instrument makers, furniture manufacturers, flooring companies, toy manufacturers, the auto industry, and some textile manufacturers that use fabrics that contain plant fibers. The 2008 amendments are expected to reduce illegal logging, which will reduce corruption and increase biodiversity and conservation in timber-supplying countries, and increase revenues for foreign and domestic companies that sell and process wood.

Legislation has been introduced in the 112th Congress to address some of the concerns with the 2008 amendments. H.R. 3210, The Retailers and Entertainers Lacey Implementation and Enforcement Fairness Act, was introduced on October 14, 2011. This bill addresses issues related to plants and plant products covered under the Lacey Act, such as declaration requirements, penalties, reporting requirements, and certification standards.[34] In addition, there was a proposed amendment to the Agriculture appropriations bill for FY2012 that would have banned funding for implementing and enforcing parts of the Lacey Act addressing plants and wildlife.[35] This would have affected efforts by APHIS, but not those of FWS and CBP, which are not funded in the Agriculture appropriations acts. The amendment was defeated.

Implementation of the 2008 Amendments

This section reviews the implementation of declaration requirements, enforcement, and funding under the 2008 amendments. Policy issues associated with implementation are discussed below in "Issues and Legislative Options."

Declaration Requirements

Under the Lacey Act, all plants or plant products being imported into the country must be declared, with some exceptions that include common cultivars, packaging material, and scientific specimens, among other things.[36] The declaration is to be made by the importer at the time of import. According to APHIS, the declaration requirements in the 2008 amendments are expected to facilitate accountability and improve data collection on plant imports.[37] Similar declaration requirements are used for the import of wildlife to the United States.

The declaration for plants and plant products is to provide:

- the scientific name of any plant (genus and species) contained in the importation;
- the value of the plant or plant product;
- the quantity of the plants or plant products (including the unit of measure); and
- the country of origin of where the plant was taken.[38]

In cases where multiple species are found in a product, there are some variations to the declaration. If a product contains material from several different plants, of which the names of the species are uncertain, the law states that the declaration should contain the names of all plant species that could have been used to create the product.[39] Furthermore, if the exact country of origin is not known, the declaration must contain the names of all of the countries from where the plant species could have come.[40] Information from submitted declarations is entered into a database, maintained by APHIS. It is unclear if this information will be openly available to the public.

The declaration does not require information on the chain of custody of the product or its parts.[41] For example, if a chair was fabricated in China with wood that was harvested and shipped from Indonesia, via Singapore, a full record of transactions throughout its fabrication process would not be necessary. The declaration will require the species of plant(s) used in the making of the chair (i.e., product imported), and the origin of each plant species used (e.g., Indonesia), and the value and quantity of the plant used. In some cases, the country of harvest for the declared plant material will be different from the country of export. The declaration requirements were to be implemented by December 2008; however, APHIS delayed implementation due to concerns about the complexity of the requirements. Consequently, the declaration requirements on certain items were implemented on a delayed schedule between April 2009 and April 2010.[42] The implementation of the declaration requirements is related to the Harmonized Tariff Schedule (HTS) of the United States, which classifies plant and plant products under certain codes in trade for duty, quota, and statistical purposes. Implementation is based on HTS codes and follows a schedule. The more complex plant products (e.g., those containing specialty wood) were to be declared by April 2010 (e.g., musical instruments). Only items classified in the current implementation schedule are subject to enforcement for compliance with the declaration schedule, according to APHIS.[43] Several other products containing wood parts, such as firearms, furniture, and toys, are being considered for phased-in implementation. As of October 2010, APHIS stated that it is not enforcing the declaration requirement for informal entries such as personal shipments. It is uncertain when or if these types of products will have to be declared.[44] Any additions to the items requiring a declaration are expected to be reported in the *Federal Register*. The 2008 amendments required a review of the declaration requirements and the effects of certain exclusions to the declaration requirements not more than two years after the enactment of the amendments (by May 22, 2010).[45] To date, this review has not been completed. However, APHIS has published a notice stating that it is initiating this review and seeking comments on the implementation of the declaration requirement.[46] Further, 180 days after the review is complete, a report reviewing the implementation of declaration requirements is to be submitted to appropriate congressional committees.[47] The report is to contain:

- an evaluation of the effectiveness of the declaration requirements in assisting enforcement of the requirements and efforts to integrate the requirements with other import regulations;
- recommendations for legislation that would assist in the identification of plants that are imported into the United States illegally; and
- an analysis of the effect of prohibitions and declaration requirements on the cost of legal plant imports and the effect on illegal logging practices and trafficking.[48]

Regulations to reflect the study's findings may be promulgated 180 days after the review discussed above.[49] The 2008 amendments authorize the regulations to include limits on the applicability of the declaration requirements to specific plant products; modifications to the requirements based on the review; and limits to the scope of the exclusions to the declaration requirement if they are warranted according to the review.

Enforcement of the Lacey Act

The Lacey Act states that the provisions and subsequent regulations under the act are to be enforced by the Secretaries of the Interior, Commerce, and in the case of plants, also the Secretary of Agriculture.[50] Agencies—for example, CBP, the US Coast Guard (e.g., for fisheries violations), the National Marine Fisheries Service, the Federal Bureau of Investigation, the US Forest Service, the Office of the Inspector General, and US Immigration and Customs Enforcement—also can enforce the Lacey Act through inspection or monitoring activities.

The Lacey Act can be enforced at the border or through investigations. Agents at ports of entry inspect imports and monitor the declaration process. Inspectors can initiate and conduct investigations into violations of the Lacey Act. The FWS Office of Law Enforcement reported 2,505 investigations related to the Lacey Act in the first nine months of 2011.[51]

Enforcement of the Lacey Act sometimes depends on an understanding of what foreign laws might have been violated. There is no federal database of foreign wildlife and plant laws, making enforcement of the law challenging.[52] However, to facilitate investigations, officials might use information gained from foreign governments, nongovernmental organizations, private citizens, anonymous tips, declarations, industry, and border agents, among others, during the investigation. Officials are also authorized to provide rewards to informants that lead to the arrest, conviction, or assessment of fines to a violator.[53]

A Lacey Act violation requires two actions to be taken. If a person violates a US or tribal law by taking, possessing, transporting, or selling any fish, wildlife, or plant (or plant product), the Lacey Act is violated if that fish, wildlife, or plant is then imported, exported, transported, sold, received, acquired, or purchased. It is slightly different for violations of state or foreign laws, which require that the import, export, transport, sale, receipt, acquisition, or purchase of the fish, wildlife, or plant be in interstate or foreign commerce before there can be a violation. A Lacey Act violation can result in civil penalties that could involve fines and forfeiture of wildlife, plants, and products, and criminal penalties that could involve fines, forfeiture, and incarceration.[54]

Funding

The Lacey Act does not authorize funding for implementing the act or enforcing provisions within the act.[55] However, funding for implementing the act can come from discretionary appropriations. The Secretary is directed to identify funds used to enforce the Lacey Act and any regulations as a special appropriations item in the Department of the Interior appropriations budget proposal to Congress.[56] Funds for implementing the act could come from other accounts in federal agencies. For example, funds for FWS investigators to enforce laws that address fish, wildlife, and plant resources are provided under the Office of Law Enforcement line item for FWS.[57] This program received $62.9 million for FY2011.

This office also funds law enforcement officials to monitor and investigate the wildlife trade. The office has 219 agents and 143 inspectors on staff for FY2012. In FY2011, investigators conducted 12,745 investigations, of which 2,505 involved cases related to the Lacey Act.[58] FWS also has an international wildlife trade program that implements domestic laws and international treaties that address the wildlife trade.[59] APHIS also funds the implementation of the Lacey Act. For example, the FY2012 budget request for APHIS requests an increase of $1.5 million to implement an electronic database to store declarations.[60]

Money taken from penalties and fines under the Lacey Act can be deposited into the Lacey Act Reward Fund. Money in this fund can be used to provide rewards to people who provide information that leads to an arrest, criminal conviction, and other things. Money can also be used to reimburse costs to those providing temporary care to fish, wildlife, or plants while a case is ongoing.[61]

Issues and Legislative Options

Several policy issues are associated with the 2008 amendments, ranging from questions about the overall purpose and function of the Lacey Act to issues about specific provisions in the act such as the declaration requirements. Several environmental, trade, and industry groups have formed coalitions to identify issues and suggest solutions. Some coalitions who primarily have issues with the declaration requirements have proposed solutions that they contend could be addressed by regulations. Others contend that the regulatory process has not worked and congressional action is needed. H.R. 3210 was introduced on October 14, 2011, to address issues related to declaration requirements, penalties, reporting requirements, and certification standards under the Lacey Act.

This section discusses selected policy issues associated with the 2008 amendments and summarizes proposed and potential legislative and regulatory options.

US Enforcement of Foreign Laws

Under the Lacey Act, the importer is responsible for making sure that imported plant and plant products are legally harvested, processed, and imported. This could involve monitoring the production of plant products and verifying that plants and plant products are being harvested, processed, and imported legally under foreign laws. This requirement has been interpreted by some as requiring the United States to enforce foreign laws, which some contend should be the responsibility of the country who established the laws. Others contend that the United States contributes to illegal trade by being one of the largest consumers of plant and plant product imports, and therefore is in a special position to apply demand-side pressure to ensure legally sourced plants and plant products for export.[62]

Some might argue that there is limited potential to lower the level of illegal trade of plants and wildlife, since the illegal trade could shift away from responsible importers (i.e., US importers following the Lacey Act) to those in countries with fewer restrictions. In the case of illegal logging, however, this argument is waning since other countries or blocks of countries are adopting regulations similar to the Lacey Act. For example, the European Union (EU) has adopted a regulation, going into effect in 2013, that will prohibit the entry of illegally harvested timber into the European market.[63] The responsibility for regulating timber will fall on those who put plant and plant products in the market (e.g., importers and producers). *Illegally harvested* is defined under the regulation as "harvested in contravention of the applicable legislation[64] in the country of harvest." The regulation applies to both timber imported into the EU and timber produced within the EU. The regulation will require that those placing timber or timber products into the market practice due diligence. Further, the regulation will require that those who buy and sell timber or timber products on the market be able to identify their suppliers and customers so that the timber and timber products can be traced.[65] If a large portion of the world market for timber adopts regulations similar to the 2008 amendments, such as the EU regulations, the market for illegally harvested or processed plants and plant products would be expected to decrease.

Addressing Laws Not Related to Conservation

Some contend that the 2008 amendments of the Lacey Act overreach the original intent of their proponents by addressing laws that are not related to conservation. For example, the act makes it unlawful to possess any plant that was processed illegally according to a foreign law.[56] As discussed in the Gibson guitar case, exporting unfinished wood conforming to HS 4407 from India is a violation of Indian law governing exports and hence a potential violation of the Lacey Act. Some could contend that illegally processing wood might not have a direct effect on conservation. Indeed, under the 2008 amendments, harvesting and exporting wood where applicable conservation laws and payment of fees and taxes are followed could still violate a country's export law (e.g., due to restrictions on unfinished wood exports) and therefore would be prohibited under the Lacey Act if the plant or plant products are imported into the United States. Counter to the argument that the Lacey Act overreaches its intent, others defend the legitimacy of the Lacey Act as a conservation tool.67 They contend that all areas covered by the Lacey Act, including export laws, have some connection to conservation. Enforcing payments of stumpage fees and taxes, for example, takes away the financial benefits of illegal logging and could provide revenue for conservation activities (e.g., more law enforcement officers). They also contend that enforcing export laws lowers the influx of illegal plants and plant products onto the market. For example, legally required processing or finishing of wood could provide another layer of oversight on the trade of plants and plant products, and could also increase the transparency of the supply chain of the plants and plant products, making enforcement of foreign laws easier.

Potential Costs and Benefits of the 2008 Amendments

The enactment and implementation of the 2008 amendments has led some to contend that the law increases costs for certain companies and could result in the loss of jobs.[68]

Others, in contrast, contend that the law increases revenue for certain companies and thus could lead to job creation.[69] There has been no comprehensive analysis of the costs and benefits of the 2008 amendments for various types of plant and plant product industries. This section discusses the potential areas of costs and benefits of the 2008 amendments.

The primary costs in complying with the 2008 amendments are attributable to exercising due care to ensure that imported plant and plant products are harvested and processed legally, and to comply with the declaration requirements. There are no published estimates of the costs to comply with the 2008 amendments.

However, the costs probably depend on the amount of due care conducted by the importer. Larger companies might have more resources to exercise due care than smaller companies. Further, those importing large quantities of wood or products from single sources might have lower costs applying due care than those purchasing small quantities of specialized wood or products from several sources.

In addition to costs associated with due care, other costs might come from complying with declaration requirements. Identifying the species and genus of wood products and filling out paperwork for declarations could require additional staff for companies importing wood and wood products. Indirect costs may result from changing trade partners that might not be able to verify the legality of their wood products. This might involve searching for new markets and establishing business with new companies. Last, there are costs associated with violations created by the 2008 amendments. Violations could result in penalties up to $500,000 for criminal violations and forfeitures of goods, which can be costly depending on the quantity and species of plants or plant products confiscated.

One of the driving forces behind the 2008 amendments is the premise that reducing illegal logging would increase revenues for legal logging operations in the United States and other countries. As discussed before, illegally logged wood is cheaper to bring to market and likely depresses wood prices for both domestic and international markets. Based on this premise, if illegally logged wood were removed from the market, prices for legally harvested wood would probably increase. According to one study, this increase could be 7%-16% annually.[70]

Less illegally harvested wood in the market could lead to an increase in the demand for legally harvested wood, causing an upward pressure on prices. To illustrate the benefits of the 2008 amendments, several cite a trade report that estimated that illegal logging contributed approximately $1 billion annually in economic losses to the US forest products industry in the form of lower exports and depressed wood prices.[71] Some contend that the revenue gained from lowering the influx of illegally harvested wood into the market could lead to more domestic jobs.[72] Another economic benefit of reducing illegal logging would be increasing revenues for governments in countries where wood is harvested. Studies have shown that illegal logging leads to corruption and evasion of paying fees and taxes for harvested and processed wood. The World Bank estimated that governments lose approximately $15 billion annually due to illegal logging, due primarily to lost revenue from taxes and fees.[73]

Declaration Requirements

The declaration requirements for plant and plant products under the 2008 amendments are controversial. Some contend that the declaration requirements are a burden and difficult to comply with under certain circumstances.[74] Others are concerned with specific parts of the declaration requirements and have suggested modifications.[75] Proponents of the declaration requirements, in general, contend that they are necessary to ensure compliance with the provisions of the Lacey Act and serve as an oversight mechanism for compliance.[76] Key points of contention and proposed solutions regarding the declaration requirements are discussed below.

Identifying Species and Genus

Some contend that wood in certain plant products is difficult to identify by genus and species.[77] For example, for composite products and materials (i.e., products that contain more than one species of wood such as particleboard), it is difficult to identify the genus and species of all the component fibers because numerous species of wood can be used to make the products. Some have suggested that these types of wood products be excluded from the declaration requirements until it is feasible to identify various fibers by species.[78] The law attempts to address complications with identifying several species of wood in products. For example, if the species of wood used in products is uncertain, one may declare all species of wood that the product could contain.[79] Therefore, if a composite wood product is created from by-products from several species, listing the species that may have been used to create the product would satisfy the declaration requirement.[80] However, APHIS has acknowledged that this might not be enough to facilitate the declaration of composite wood, and has asked for information on this issue to consider regulatory options.[81] In the request for comments for potential changes in regulations, APHIS proposes a definition for composite wood and identifies two possible approaches for declaring composite wood through regulations. APHIS would define composite wood as consisting of plant material that has been chemically or mechanically broken down and reconstituted. The approaches to declaring composite wood would involve applying a type of *de minimis*[82] standard to the wood. One approach is to identify the genus, species, and country of harvest for no less than a given percentage of the wood contained in the product. The percentage could be measured in terms of weight or volume. The second approach would be to declare the "average percent composite plant content" of the product, without regard for the species and country of harvest for the plant. Non-composite plant material would still need the genus, species, and country of harvest in the declaration. A *de minimis* standard has also been proposed for certain types of products that contain plant materials which are highly processed and are in small quantities.[83] Some argue that identifying these plant materials is difficult due to the level of processing they have undergone and their small quantity in the product. Under this proposal, plant materials in certain products would be excluded from the declaration requirements. Product examples include cosmetics, personal care products, textiles, and rubber or cork products. Proponents of this proposal contend that federal agencies have rulemaking authority to make these exclusions, but that congressional action might be needed to clarify the agency's authority to establish exclusions to the declaration requirements.[84]

H.R. 3210 addresses this issue regarding composite wood by exempting all non-solid wood plant products derived from a tree from declaration requirements under the act.[85] Section 3(a) of H.R. 3210 would appear to exclude composite woods, paper, and particleboard, among others, from declaration requirements. The bill would also require APHIS to issue regulations that would define the term "solid wood" to clarify the exclusions.[86]

Some counter the need for modifications to the declaration requirements because they contend that knowing the type and source of wood is important for ensuring legal practices and countering the illegal trade.[87] They specifically oppose provisions in H.R. 3210 that broaden the exemptions of plant products from declaration requirements, arguing that provisions under H.R. 3210 would exclude pulp and paper, which constitute a significant portion of the plant imports into the United States, from declaration requirements.[88]

Blanket Declarations

Some contend that repeated or regular declarations of the same plant products add administrative burden and extra costs on industries without providing additional benefits for tracing the source of wood.[89] A proposal to address this issue would allow for a blanket declaration.[90] In a blanket declaration, importers would submit one declaration for similar products imported over a period of time, thus potentially saving the importer from submitting duplicate declarations for each product imported. APHIS has responded to this issue by initiating the Lacey Act Blanket Declaration Pilot Program in 2009 to test the feasibility of collecting information through a blanket declaration. [91] Eligible importers can participate in the program.[92] A blanket declaration will apply for one month, and a reconciliation report providing how much was actually imported during the month is due within 15 days after the end of the month.

The modification of declaration requirements can be done either through regulations or by law. As discussed above, H.R. 3210 includes provisions to change the declaration requirements. Regulatory changes to the declaration requirements under the Lacey Act can be implemented from recommendations provided by certain reports and reviews. As discussed above, under the Lacey Act, the Secretary[93] is required to review the declaration requirements and report findings to appropriate congressional committees.[94] The report to Congress is to contain information on several factors, including an evaluation of the effectiveness of declaration requirements. The Secretary is authorized to promulgate regulations that could modify certain declaration requirements for plant products 180 days after the Secretary completes the review.[95] For example, the Secretary could limit the applicability of declaration requirements to any plant product; make changes to declaration requirements for plant products that are suggested in the review; and limit the scope of exclusions if they are justified by the review.[96] This could be an avenue for excluding products (e.g., composite wood products) that are difficult to declare. It is unclear, however, if these regulations could be used to exempt plant products made before 2008 from the declaration process.

Excluding Plant and Plant Products Imported or Compiled before 2008

Some contend that the 2008 amendments should not apply to plants imported or plant products created or imported before 2008.[97] They note that declaration requirements under the act are difficult to complete for these plant products because the sources and species of plants used might not be known, since they were not required by law to be identified.[98] This issue is addressed in H.R. 3210, which proposes to exclude plants from the Lacey Act that were imported into the United States before May 2008 or plant products created before May 2008.[99] The intent of this provision in H.R. 3210 appears to be to exclude *plant products* created and imported before 2008 from Lacey Act coverage and clarify any doubts or interpretations of the law.[100] Note that this provision would not cover plants harvested before 2008 that were also not imported before the act took effect, making them still subject to the Lacey Act.

H.R. 3210 would also limit the types of wood that require a declaration. Wood “entered for consumption” would be subjected to declaration requirements.[101] The bill specifically cites 19 C.F.R. §141.0a for a definition of *entered for consumption*. Under this regulation, *entered for consumption* applies to wood that is considered merchandise and has an entry summary for consumption filed with CBP. The intent of this provision appears to be to exclude those plant products or plants intended for personal use (e.g., musical instruments) from the declaration requirements.

Exercising Due Care

The primary method by which US importers can protect themselves from criminal and certain civil penalties under the Lacey Act is to exercise due care in determining if the imported plants or plant products were legally harvested, processed, and exported. The exercise of due care refers to the amount of attention and effort that a reasonable person would expend in a similar situation to address an issue or conduct an activity. Some contend that the actions needed to demonstrate due care with respect to the Lacey Act are not sufficiently defined or clear.[102] Some definitions of due care are found in S.Rept. 97-123, which accompanied the Lacey Act amendments of 1981, and in guidance provided by federal agencies. S.Rept. 97-123 describes due care thus: “Briefly stated, due care means that degree of care which a reasonably prudent person would exercise under the same or similar circumstances.”[103] Further, the Senate report notes that due care requires that a person under certain circumstances take steps that a reasonable person would take under similar circumstances to insure they are not violating the law.[104]

The exercise of due care is pivotal for determining penalties under the Lacey Act. Under the Lacey Act, certain civil and criminal violations and forfeitures can be imposed on persons if they engaged in conduct prohibited by the act. If they knowingly engaged in prohibited conduct, the penalties are steeper than if they unknowingly engaged in prohibited conduct. If they unknowingly committed a violation without exercising due care, their penalties are steeper than if they exercised due care and unknowingly committed a violation. (See *Figure 1*.) Therefore, persons who exercise sufficient due care to determine if their plants or plant products were taken, possessed, transported, or sold in violation of laws, treaties, or regulations might not be held liable for certain violations under the act if a violation is committed unknowingly.[105] However, exercising due care and unknowingly committing a violation could still result in penalties under the Lacey Act, such as forfeiting goods.[106] The due care standard does not apply to marking or labeling violations, and is excluded from declaration requirements under the Lacey Act.

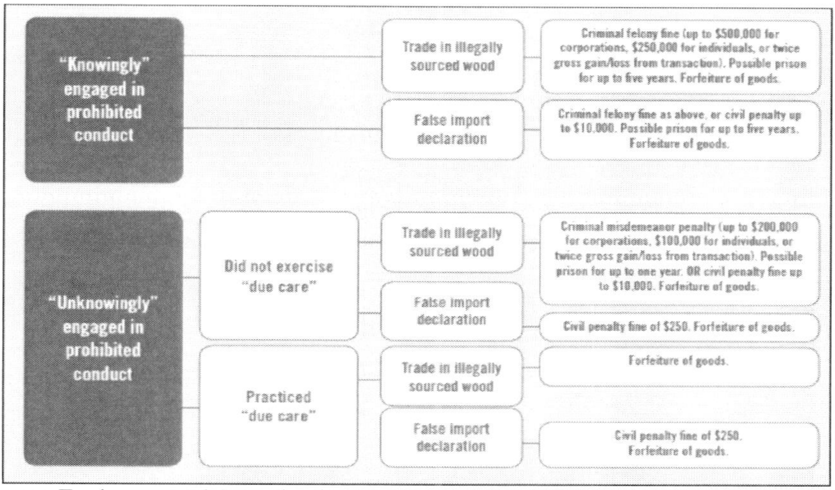

Source: Environmental Investigation Agency, The US Lacey Act: Frequently Asked Questions About the World's First Ban on Trade in Illegal Wood, Environmental Investigation Agency, January 2009, http://www.eia-global.org/PDF/ EIA.Lacey Report.English.pdf.

Figure 1. Summary of Penalties Under the Lacey Act.

According to S.Rept. 97-123, the intent behind incorporating a due care standard in the Lacey Act was to lower the potential for abusive and indiscriminate enforcement efforts.[107] The Senate report also notes that the degree of due care is "applied differently to different categories of persons with varying degrees of knowledge and responsibility."[108] For example, a horticulturalist in a professional capacity and with experience in the plant trade could be expected to apply greater knowledge toward correctly identifying plants and verifying permits than would be expected of an airline company that transported plants to the United States and has little knowledge of the plant trade and plant species. Some practical measures one could take to demonstrate due care are given by APHIS.[109] For example, importers can ask questions about the chain of custody of the wood, implement compliance plans, abide by industry standards, record efforts at each stage of the supply chain, and change their practices in response to practical experiences. Some red flags that might indicate violations of logging or processing laws offered by APHIS include:

- goods trading significantly below their common market rate;
- cash transactions without paperwork;
- invalid or falsified documents or permits; and
- unusual sales practices or transactions.

Process for Exercising Due Care

Establishing a process for exercising due care under the Lacey Act when dealing with plants and plant products has been proposed for clarifying guidelines. Some suggest that a process for exercising due care should have steps a person or company can take to verify that their imported plants and plant products comply with the Lacey Act, ultimately leading to a type of certification for the plant or plant product. For example, H.R. 3210 would direct selected federal agency heads responsible for implementing the Lacey Act to establish a standard certification process for plant and plant products legally harvested, imported, or manufactured after May 2008.[110] The process could consider certification of individual items as well as certification of manufacturers, importers, and retailers. Others are also considering a process for satisfying due care. A group of stakeholders associated with the trade of plants and plant products and conservation are creating a process that aims to define due care under the Lacey Act.[111] The effort is ongoing and, to date, no publically available proposals or drafts of the standard are available.

A process for exercising due care has been adopted by the European Union (EU) in regulations that aim to curb illegal logging.[112] The process has three primary elements that are to be provided:

- Information on the timber and timber products, including a description and scientific name of the timber, country of harvest, quantity of the timber or product, details on the supplier and purchaser, and documents indicating compliance with national legislation.
- A risk assessment of the timber being illegal throughout its supply chain based on information gathered and risk assessment criteria, which include compliance with applicable legislation, prevalence of illegal logging of specific species in the country of harvest, international sanctions on imports of timber, and complexity of the supply chain.
- Risk mitigation addressing the risks noted in the previous point, which can include gathering additional information and verification of

legality from the supplier of the timber, including obtaining third party verification. [113]

The regulation also provides for monitoring organizations to be recognized.[114] These organizations are expected to provide EU operators due care systems, which they can accept or refuse in lieu of creating their own system. The EU system for due diligence is similar to the 2008 amendments, but potentially more involved. Under the EU system, information on the chain of custody and a calculation for mitigating risks is required; this information is not required under the 2008 amendments. Clarity on how to exercise due care and a defense against charges when due care is exercised are two potential benefits of implementing a process for exercising due care. A process that specifies steps to ensure the legality of imported products would reduce confusion as to how due care is exercised, and provide consistent practices among importers, thus making it easier for them to coordinate efforts to verify the legality of their products. This could also lower the costs of compliance. Further, monitoring compliance according to a process could give law enforcement officials a benchmark for bringing charges against an importer who may not have taken sufficient steps to exercise due care. Potential drawbacks of establishing and implementing a process to exercise due care include determining the level of reliability for verifying timber practices in foreign countries and the potential for violations to go unnoticed when due care is applied. One component of a due care process might be employing third parties to verify timber operations in foreign countries (i.e., certification scheme). Third parties can invest resources in particular countries to monitor logging and processing operations for several importers, and provide a certificate to operations that comply with the law. For example, the Forest Stewardship Council (FSC) certifies timber operations to ensure legal, sustainable management of forested land and monitors the chain of custody to trace the life cycle of wood products originating in a certified forest.[115] The effectiveness of third parties to monitor all aspects of plant harvesting and production, however, has been questioned by some. They claim that corruption and fraud can take place, thus undercutting the ability to certify legal wood.[116] This would lower the credibility of the standard and lower its effect in curbing illegal logging. Further, some certification schemes might not cover all aspects of a due care process and the timber and timber products in question. FSC, for example, does not apply rigorous oversight to "FSC Controlled Wood," which is non-FSCcertified wood that is allowed to be mixed with FSC-certified wood.[117] Further, certification schemes may not cover all steps in the succession from harvesting to importation. For example, FSC standards would not cover some laws dealing with the export or processing of wood after harvest that would be subject to the Lacey Act.[118]

Foreign Laws

Exercising due care for importing plant and plant products under the Lacey Act can be challenging for importers because it requires an understanding of foreign laws and practices, and possibly monitoring in the foreign country where plant and plant materials are being harvested. Some contend that exercising due care is complicated by the quantity of foreign laws related to plants and plant products. For example, Indonesia has more than 900 laws, regulations, and decrees that address timber harvesting and processing.[119] There is no federal database that compiles and presents foreign laws that apply to plants and plant products. According to APHIS, importers are responsible for being aware of any foreign laws that apply to the plant and plant products they are importing.[120] This issue is addressed in H.R. 3210, which states in its findings that federal agencies have the responsibility to provide a public database that contains foreign laws that apply to the importation of plants.[121] H.R. 3210 contains a provision that directs the Director of FWS to submit an evaluation of the feasibility of creating and maintaining a database of foreign laws of countries where plants are imported.[122]

Options for Improving the Exercise of Due Care

Some have suggested other options for reducing illegal logging that would help importers exercise due care.[123] These options would be supply-side driven. One option is to encourage timber-producing countries to construct timber legality standards that could be implemented as voluntary guidelines or mandatory procedures for domestic timber operations. Supply-side guidelines were implemented in a trade agreement between the United States and Peru in 2006 to address illegal logging in Peru. [124] For example, Peru is required to implement several measures to deter illegal logging within the country, such as increasing the number of enforcement personnel, imposing criminal and civil penalties under existing laws to deter illegal logging, monitoring endangered plant species, verifying and auditing exporters and producers of timber products, and developing tools that strengthen regulatory controls and verification systems related to the harvest and trade of timber products. Individual countries have also initiated legality standards to differentiate between legal and illegal sources of wood.[125] Indonesia, for example, has a standard with several indicators that address timber operations and forest management. Independent auditors assess timber concessions and factories against the standard and award certificates for legal operations. Another option is to promote international cooperation and coordination to identify areas of legal and illegal logging practices. With the advent of the EU regulation, opportunities exist for coordination among a large range of importers spanning two of the largest markets for plant and plant product exports—Europe and North America. Efforts could be made to identify "hot spots" where illegal logging is common, as well as areas where legal practices prevail. This could create incentives for suppliers to be placed on the legal lists. Further, identifying areas where illegal logging or trade exists could warn importers of areas in their supply chain they should be wary about. This might also encourage importers to change their supply chains so as to avoid these areas. However, these lists could be subjectively created and generate controversy by countries that are on the list. For example, some might question how many infractions would cause a country to be listed, or how a country could come off the list. Legal operators in the listed country might also argue that they are being unfairly targeted because of the crimes of others in their country. Some have suggested strengthening existing federal programs aimed at reducing illegal logging in foreign countries as a mechanism to make compliance with the Lacey Act easier.[126] Some examples include programs at the US Agency of International Development and Department of State that aim to educate foreign companies about the Lacey Act and provide funds to improve forest governance and law enforcement in foreign countries. An example is the Tropical Forest Conservation Act.[127] Under this program, debt restructured in eligible countries generates funds to support programs to conserve tropical forests within the debtor country. Some of the eligible activities include improving law enforcement capacity in reserves to address illegal logging. This helps importers by reducing illegal logging practices in countries that supply plants and plant products.

CONCLUDING REMARKS

Some aspects of the 2008 Lacey Act Amendments have been controversial, and several observers and stakeholders have suggested potential changes. Some contend that changes to should be done through law; others argue that changes should be done through regulations. Proponents of H.R. 3210 state that efforts to change the implementation of the Lacey Act through regulations have stalled and not produced results.[128] This is supported, in part, by the delay by APHIS in producing a review report of implementing declaration requirements under the act. Based on this report, the Secretary is authorized to make certain changes to the declaration requirements. Proponents of making changes through regulations contend that amending the act could lead to additional changes in the law that are not contemplated or supported by various stakeholders. They also contend that amending the law is subverting the intended process of making changes through regulations.[129]

End Notes

[1] For example, prior to the act, hunters would kill game in one state illegally and transport it to another state where they could sell it legally. When the game was transported out of its state of origin, that state did not have the jurisdiction to prosecute the hunter in another state where the game was sold. The state where the sale took place generally did not have laws prohibiting the sale of game illegally taken in another state. Robert Anderson, "The Lacey Act: America's Premier Weapon in the Fight Against Unlawful Wildlife Trafficking," Public Land Law Review, vol. 16, no. 27 (1995), p. 38.

[2] A person includes any individual, partnership, association, corporation, trust, or any officer, employee, agent, department, or instrumentality of the federal government or of any state or political subdivision, or any other entity subject to the jurisdiction of the United States.

[3] This was in the US code before amendments in 2008 at 16 USC. §3372(a). The term plant refers to only indigenous plants of any state that are listed pursuant to any state law promoting the conservation of the species or under the Convention on International Trade in Endangered Species of Wild Fauna and Flora.

[4] 16 USC. §§3372(a)(2)-(3).

[5] 16 USC. §§3372(a)(1)-(4). For a detailed description of the 2008 amendments to the Lacey Act, including prohibitions related to plants and penalties related to civil and criminal violations, see CRS Report R42067, The Lacey Act: Protecting the Environment by Restricting Trade, by Kristina Alexander.

[6] 16 USC. §3372(a)(1).

[7] 16 USC. §§3372(d) and (f).

[8] 16 USC. §3371(f)(1).

[9] 16 USC. §3371(f)(2).

[10] For plant products, the declaration requirements could be modified if the species and country of origin varies and is unknown. In these cases, all of the species that may have been used and all of the countries where the plants may have been taken are to be identified, as discussed below. Packaging supplies that contain plant material are excluded from declaration requirements.

[11] For example, wood harvested in Brazil before 2008 would need to have declaration forms if it was imported into the country now.

[12] For example, see US Congress, House Committee on Natural Resources, Legal Timber Protection Act, report to accompany H.R. 1497, 110th Cong., 2nd sess., September 24, 2008, H.Rept. 110-882 (Washington: GPO, 2008) pp. 3-4.

[13] "Hardwoods" is a term commonly used for trees in the phylum Anthophyta (angiosperms, or flowering plants), because the dominant hardwood tree species of temperate climates (oaks and maples) are harder (more dense) than the major "softwood" species (pines, firs, and spruces), trees of the order Coniferales (conifers). However, some "hardwood" species (e.g., aspen and poplar) are much softer (less dense) than many "softwoods." In this report, "hardwood" is used to indicate angiosperms, while "softwood" (or conifer) is used for coniferous species.

[14] Seneca Creek Associates, LLC, and Wood Resources International, LLC, "Illegal" Logging and Global Wood Markets: The Competitive Impacts on the US Wood Products Industry, prepared for American Forest & Paper Association (November 2004), 154 pp. Hereinafter known as Illegal Logging and Global Markets.

[15] For example, logging illegally within designated park boundaries could lead to environmental impacts such as habitat alteration and loss of biodiversity; also, evading fees and royalties could reduce revenues to governments, which might result in lower funds for conservation activities.

[16] World Bank, A Revised Forest Strategy for the World Bank Group (Washington, DC: October 31, 2002), p. 12.

[17] Shadia Duery and Richard P. Vlosky, US Demand for Certified Tropical Hardwood Products: The Supply Chain Perspective, Lousiana Forest Products Development Center, Working Paper #78, November 15, 2006, pp. 1-14.

[18] Natural Resources Defense Council, Trade in Bigleaf Mahogany: The Need for Strict Implementation of CITES (September 2006), available at http://docs.nrdc.org/international/files/int_06100201a.pdf.

[19] Illegal Logging and Global Markets, p. ES-2.

[20] Illegal Logging and Global Markets, p. ES-2.

[21] Illegal Logging and Global Markets, p. 26.

[22] John M. Rayfield, US Fish and Wildlife Service, Affidavit in Support of Search Warrant # 11-MJ-1067 A, B, C, D, p. 4 (Aug. 18, 2011), hereafter Affidavit.

[23] Affidavit, p. 3. In general, smuggling laws under 18 USC. §545 make it unlawful to knowingly import or bring merchandise into the United States contrary to law, or to receive, conceal, sell, or facilitate the transportation of such merchandise after importation, knowing that the merchandise was brought into the United States contrary to law.

[24] Affidavit, pp. 8 and 14.

[25] The HS implemented in the Harmonized Tariff Schedule (HTS) of the United States. An HS or HTS code is assigned to a set of products with stated characteristics.

[26] Veneer is generally a thin decorative covering of fine wood applied to a coarser wood or other material. For example, under HS 4408, veneer is defined as being not more than 6 mm thick.

[27] Affidavit, p. 7.

[28] Tariff classification ruling NY 881630 (January 26, 1993), pertaining to sawn Indian rosewood (Dalbergia latifolia) and sawn Indian ebony (Diospyros ebenum).

[29] Affidavit, p. 12.

[30] For example, see Bill DiBenedetto, "Farm Bill's Illegal Logging Ban Hits Shippers, Logistics Companies," Journal of Commerce, August 8, 2008, p. 1.

[31] Consensus Statement of Importers, Non-Governmental Organizations, and Domestic Producers on Lacey Act Clarifications, July 17, 2009. See http://www.troutmansandersnews. Com /marcom/news/TS-Intl_Trade_2009-07-17.pdf. Hereinafter referred to as Consensus Statement.

[32] Consensus Statement.

[33] For example, see Jake Schmidt, "Lacey Act: The Diverse Coalition that Supports It and Why Efforts to Weaken It Should be Resisted," Switchboard, October 3, 2011, http://switch board.nrdc.org/blogs/jschmidt/ lacey_act_the_diverse_coalitio.html. Hereinafter "Lacey Act: The Diverse Coalition That Supports It and Why Efforts to Weaken It Should be Resisted."

[34] For a section-by-section summary of the legislation, see CRS Report R42067, The Lacey Act: Protecting the Environment by Restricting Trade, by Kristina Alexander.

[35] S.Amdt. 765 to H.R. 2112 (112th Congress).

[36] 16 USC. §3372(f).

[37] APHIS, Lacey Act Amendments, Complete List of Questions and Answers, October 19, 2010, http://www.aphis.usda.gov/plant_health/lacey_act/downloads/faq.pdf. Hereinafter Lacey Act Amendments, Complete List of Questions and Answers.

[38] 16 USC. §3372(f)(1).

[39] 16 USC. §3372(f)(2)(A).

[40] 16 USC. §3372(f)(2)(B).

[41] In this context, chain of custody is the location and handlers of the plant and plant product during its harvest and fabrication until it gets to the importer.

[42] See 74 Fed. Reg. 45415 (September 2, 2009).

[43] Lacey Act Amendments, Complete List of Questions and Answers, #11.

[44] Lacey Act Amendments, Complete List of Questions and Answers, #12.

[45] 16 USC. §3372(f)(4).

[46] 76 Fed. Reg. 10874 (Feb. 28, 2011).

[47] 16 USC. §3372(f)(5).

[48] 16 USC. §3372(f)(5).

[49] 16 USC. §3372(f)(6).

[50] 16 USC. §3375(a).

[51] This refers to all aspects of the Lacey Act, including fish and wildlife, and plants. US Fish and Wildlife Service, Office of Law Enforcement, "Law Enforcement at a Glance," press release, September 2011.

[52] Lacey Act Amendments, Complete List of Questions and Answers, #8.

[53] 16 USC. §3375(d).

[54] For further discussion of penalties under the Lacey Act, see CRS Report R42067, The Lacey Act: Protecting the Environment by Restricting Trade, by Kristina Alexander.

[55] Activities authorized under law can be funded by appropriations without an authorization.

[56] 16 USC. §3378(e).

[57] US Fish and Wildlife Service, US Fish and Wildlife Service Fiscal Year 2012 Budget Justifications, Department of the Interior, Budget Justification, Washington, DC, 2011, p. LE-5.

[58] Office of Law Enforcement, Law Enforcement at a Glance, US Fish and Wildlife Service, Public Information, Washington, DC, September 2011, pp. 1-2.

[59] This program also implements the Convention on International Trade in Endangered Species of Wild Fauna and Flora (CITES), and processes and organizes permits and trade records. For more information, see CRS Report RL32751, The Convention on International Trade in Endangered Species of Wild Fauna and Flora (CITES): Background and Issues, by Pervaze A. Sheikh and M. Lynne Corn.

[60] USDA, "2012 Explanatory Notes, APHIS," p. 18-39, http://www.obpa.usda.gov /18aphis 2012notes.pdf.

[61] 16 USC. §3375(d).

[62] "Lacey Act: The Diverse Coalition That Supports It and Why Efforts to Weaken it Should be Resisted."

[63] EU Timber Regulation (Regulation (EU) No 995/2010).

[64] Applicable foreign legislation covers rights to harvest timber within legal boundaries; payments for rights and taxes related to harvesting; environmental and forest legislation applicable directly to timber harvesting; legal rights of third parties as it applies to land use and tenure affected by timber harvesting; and trade and customs laws related to the forest sector. EU Timber Regulation (Regulation (EU) No 995/2010), Article 2(g)-(h).

[65] Jon Buckrell and Alison Hoare, Controlling Illegal Logging: Implementation of the EU Timber Regulation, Chatham House, Briefing Paper, June 2011, http://www.chathamhouse.org/sites/default/files/0611buckrell_hoare.pdf.

[66] 16 USC. §3372(a)(3)(B)(iii).

[67] "Lacey Act: The Diverse Coalition That Supports It and Why Efforts to Weaken It Should be Resisted."

[68] For references to jobs, see letter from Hon. Fred Upton, Chairman of the Committee on Energy and Commerce et al. to Hon. Daniel Ash, Director of the US Fish and Wildlife Service, et al., September 8, 2011, http://republicans.energycommerce.house.gov/Media/file/Letters/090811%20Letter%20to%20DOJ%20Interior%20Fish%20and%20Wildlife.pdf.

[69] For example, see Rep. Earl Blumenauer, "Lacey Act Protects American Jobs," House of Representatives, Congressional Record, vol. 157, part 141 (September 21, 2011), pp. H6276-H6277 and Heath Combs, "Business Owners Say Lacey Act Can Save Jobs," Furniture Today, September 26, 2011, p. 1, http://www.furnituretoday.com/ article/543612-Business_Owners_Say_Lacey_Act_Can_Save_Jobs.php.

[70] Illegal Logging and Global Wood Markets, p. ES-2. Higher prices could be a potential negative consequence for consumers who might have to pay more for wood. This could affect a different set of domestic companies.

[71] Illegal Logging and Global Wood Markets, p. 26.

[72] Letter from American Forest Foundation et al. to Member of Congress, October 11, 2011.

[73] World Bank, A Revised Forest Strategy for the World Bank Group (Washington, DC: October 31, 2002).

[74] Consensus Statement.

[75] Consensus Statement.

[76] In relation to removing declaration requirements for non-solid wood products, see letter from Blue Green Alliance et al. to Members of Congress, November 1, 2011, http://climateadvisers.com/pdf/ Oppose%20RELIEF%20Act%20Letter.pdf. Hereafter Blue Green Alliance Letter.

[77] Consensus Statement.

[78] Consensus Statement.

[79] 16 USC. §3372(f)(2)(A).

[80] Lacey Act Amendments, Complete List of Questions and Answers, #18.

[81] Animal Plant and Health Inspection Service, "Implementation of Revised Lacey Act Revisions," 76 Fed. Reg. 38330-38332, June 30, 2011.

[82] De minimis broadly refers to an insignificant or negligible quantity of something. In reference to this situation, a de minimis quantity of plant material would be considered negligible or small enough that it would not require a declaration.

[83] American Apparel & Footwear Association et al., Second Consensus Statement of Importers, Non-governmental Organizations, and Domestic Producers on Lacey Act Clarifications, June 23, 2010, p. 2. Hereafter, the Second Consensus Statement.

[84] Second Consensus Statement, p. 2.

[85] H.R. 3210, §3(a).

[86] H.R. 3210, §3(a).

[87] Blue Green Alliance Letter.

[88] Ibid.

[89] Consensus Statement.

[90] Consensus Statement.

[91] See the description at APHIS Lacey Act Blanket Declaration Pilot Program, http://www.aphis.usda.gov/plant_health/ lacey_act/downloads/Instructions.pdf.

[92] Eligible importers include those participating in one of two expedited border release programs, the Automated Line Release Program or the Border Release Advance Screening and Selectivity Program.

[93] When it pertains to plants, the Secretary under the Lacey Act refers to the Secretary of the Interior or Commerce, and the Secretary of Agriculture.

[94] 16 USC. §3372(f)(4).

[95] 16 USC. §3372(f)(6).

[96] 16 USC. §3372(f)(6).

[97] For example, see Consensus Statement.

[98] For example, see §2(8) of H.R. 3210.

[99] H.R. 3210, §3(a).

[100] Congressman Jim Cooper, "The RELIEF Act: Frequently Asked Questions," press release, October 20, 2011, http://cooper.house.gov/index.php?option=com_content&task =view&id =538&Itemid=76.

[101] H.R. 3210, §3(a).

[102] Jim Gould, Continuing Wood Trade Under the Lacey Act Amendments, Floor Covering Institute, White Paper, pp. 1- 6, http://floorcoveringinstitute.com/files/ Lacey__Act__ Article15_2.pdf.

[103] US Congress, Senate Committee on Environment and Public Works, Lacey Act Amendments of 1981, Senate report to accompany S.736, 97th Cong., 1st sess., April 27, 1981, S. Rept. 97-123 (Washington: GPO, May 21, 1981), p. 10.

[104] Ibid.

[105] 16 USC. §§3373-3374.

[106] For more on violations and penalties under the Lacey Act, see CRS Report R42067, The Lacey Act: Protecting the Environment by Restricting Trade, by Kristina Alexander.

[107] For a more detailed explanation of the due care standard and how it applies to violations under the Lacey Act, see CRS Report R42067, The Lacey Act: Protecting the Environment by Restricting Trade, by Kristina Alexander.

[108] S.Rept. 97-123, p. 10.

[109] Gary Lougee, Lacey Act Primer, Animal and Plant Health Inspection Services, Power Point, April 2010, http://www.aphis.usda.gov/plant_health/lacey_act/downloads/LaceyAct Primer. pdf.

[110] H.R. 3210, §7.

[111] National Association of Music Merchants, "NAMM Joins Lacey Act Defense National Consensus Committee," press release, October 27, 2011, http://www.prnewswire. com/

news-releases/namm-joins-lacey-act-defense-nationalconsensus-committee-132769818.html.

[112] European Union Regulation No. 995/2010, http://eur-lex.europa.eu/LexUri Serv/ LexUri Serv.do?uri=OJ:L:2010:295:0023:0034:EN:PDF. This process is referred to as a due diligence system and is planned to take effect in 2013.

[113] European Union Regulation No. 995/2010, Article 6.

[114] European Union Regulation No 995/2010, Article 8.

[115] For more on forest certification and potential issues, see CRS Report R41992, Forest Certification Programs, by Ross W. Gorte.

[116] Frederic Achard et al., Vital Forest Graphics, United Nations Environment Programme/GRID-Arendal, 2009, pp. 54-56, http://www.grida.no/files/publications/ vital_ forest_graphics.pdf.

[117] Forest Stewardship Council, "FSC Controlled Wood," http://www.fsc.org/cw.html. The FSC controlled wood must still not originate from wood that was harvested illegally, in violation of civil rights, in forests with high conservation values, from the conversion of natural forests, or from areas where genetically modified trees have been planted.

[118] Although Gibson has bought FSC-certified wood in the past, the 2011 Lacey Act violation against Gibson addressed an Indian law related to finishing wood before export. The finishing process is not covered by FSC certification.

[119] Rachel Saltzman, "Establishing a 'Due Care' Standard Under the Lacey Act Amendments of 2008," Michigan Law Review First Impressions, vol. 109, no. 1 (2010), pp. 1-8, http://www.michiganlawreview.org/assets/fi/109/ saltzman.pdf. Hereinafter "Establishing a "Due Care" Standard Under the Lacey Act Amendments of 2008."

[120] Lacey Act Amendments, Complete List of Questions and Answers, #8.

[121] H.R. 3210, §1(11).

[122] H.R. 3210, §5.

[123] "Establishing a 'Due Care' Standard Under the Lacey Act Amendments of 2008," p. 6.

[124] United States-Peru Trade Promotion Agreement, Chapter 18, Environment, at http://www.ustr.gov/ Trade_Agreements/Bilateral/Peru_TPA/Final_Texts/Section_Index.html.

[125] "Establishing a 'Due Care' Standard Under the Lacey Act Amendments of 2008," p. 6.

[126] Environmental Investigation Agency (EIA), The US Lacey Act: Tackling the Illegal Trade in Timber, Plants, and Wood Products, Funding for Implementation in FY2012, 2011, pp. 1-4, http://www.eia-global.org/ forests_for_the_world/lacey.html.

[127] CRS Report RL31286, Debt-for-Nature Initiatives and the Tropical Forest Conservation Act: Status and Implementation, by Pervaze A. Sheikh.

[128] Congressman Jim Cooper, "The RELIEF Act: Frequently Asked Questions," press release, 2011, http://cooper.house.gov/index.php?option =com_content&task=view&id=538& Item id=76.

[129] Blue Green Alliance Letter.

In: The Lacey Act
Editors: G. E. Morgan and D. Hill

ISBN 978-1-62081-615-8

Chapter 3

LACEY ACT AMENDMENT: COMPLETE LIST OF QUESTIONS AND ANSWERS*

United States Department of Agriculture, Animal and Plant Health Inspection Service

GENERAL QUESTIONS

1. When Were the Amendments Effective?

The Lacey Act amendments included in the 2008 Farm Bill were effective as of May 22, 2008. As a practical matter, this means that enforcement actions may be taken for any violations committed on or after that date. The requirement to provide a declaration under the amended Act went into effect May 1, 2009.

The most recent phase of the implementation began Aprill, 2010, at which point all products on the revised schedule require a declaration. To view the phase-in schedule, see: http://www.aphis.usda.gov/plant health/lacey act/ downloads/ImplementationSchedule.pdf.

* This is an edited, reformatted and augmented version of the United States Department of Agriculture Animal and Plant Health Inspection Service Plant Protection and Quarantine publication, dated February 16, 2012.

2. What Is Considered a "Plant" under the Lacey Act?

Under the Lacey Act, as amended, "Plant" means: "Any wild member of the plant kingdom, including roots, seeds, parts or product thereof, and including trees from either natural or planted forest stands." There are some exclusions.

Common cultivars (except trees) and common food crops are excluded from the definition of plant. In addition, a scientific specimen of plant genetic material that is to be used only for laboratory or field research and any plant that is to remain planted or to be planted or replanted is also excluded from the definition of plant, unless the plant is listed under the Endangered Species Act or a similar State law, or is listed in an appendix to the Convention on International Trade in Endangered Species of Wild Fauna and Flora (CITES).

3. Why Does Lacey Now Cover "Any Wild Member of the Plant Kingdom" (Excluding Common Food Crops and Common Cultivars)? Are There Plant Products (Other Than Timber and Timber Products) Where Illegal Harvest and Associated Trade Is a Concern?

Although considerable recent attention has been focused on illegal logging and associated trade, other wild plants also face the threat of illegal harvesting. Prior to the recent amendments,

Lacey Act protections covered only endangered plants (such as those listed on appendixes of CITES), and there were prosecutions involving the illegal harvest and associated trade of non-timber plants species such as orchids, ginseng, saguaro cacti, and others.

4. Will Regulations Be Developed?

The Lacey Act amendments include specific provisions for the promulgation of regulations including to define the terms "common food crop" and "common cultivar" and to limit the exclusion of packaging material from the declaration requirements, if warranted. However, most of the statute is self-implementing and thus may be enforced prior to the issuance of any implementing regulations.

5. What Is the Purpose of the Declaration Requirement?

Congress did not set forth within the Act an official purpose of the declaration requirement. Declarations generally serve several purposes including but not limited to data acquisition and accountability. Prior to the recent amendments, the Lacey Act already required similar declarations for imports (as well as exports) of wildlife.

6. Where Can I Find a List of Plants Prohibited under the Lacey Act?

The Lacey Act pertains to plants (in particular trees) that are illegally harvested. There is no list of specifically prohibited plants under the Lacey Act because the Act applies to all plants, as defined in the statute (see question #2).

7. Where Can I Find Scientific Names For Plants?

The following websites may be useful to look-up the scientific names of plants:

- http://www.ars-grin.gov/cgi-bin/npgs/html/tax_search.pl
- http://plants.usda.gov
- http://www.itis.gov/
- http://www.ipni.org/

8. Is There a Database of Foreign Laws That Will Be Enforced As a Result of the Lacey Act Amendment?

The Lacey Act now makes it unlawful to import, export, transport, sell, receive, acquire, or purchase in interstate or foreign commerce any plant, with some limited exceptions, taken, possessed, transported or sold in violation of the laws of the United States, a State, an Indian tribe, or any foreign law that protects plants or that regulates certain plant related offenses. It is the responsibility of the importer to be aware of any foreign laws that may pertain to their merchandise prior to its importation into the United States. Currently, the US Government has no plans to create such a database.

9. Is There a De Minimis Exception?

The statute does not provide for any de minimis exceptions, either to the substantive prohibitions or to the declaration requirement. However, the relative amount of an item at issue may be a factor in enforcement as it may go to the issue of knowledge and/or due care.

For example, violations of the declaration requirements must be knowing before there is any criminal violation under the statute; there is no due care misdemeanor for violation of the declaration requirement. Where a very small amount of product is found to be in a shipment but not in a declaration, it may indicate a circumstance in which the declaration was not knowingly false, and thus not a criminal violation.

And, as with any other customs declaration requirements (e.g., product description, weight, value, etc.) violations, enforcement agencies may exercise discretion on any potential penalties depending upon the severity of the incident.

10. How Will Affected Importers/Industries Be Kept Informed about Information Pertaining to the Lacey Act?

APHIS will continue to provide the latest information regarding the Lacey Act on our Web site, http://www.aphis.usda.gov/plant_health/lacey_act . We also encourage persons interested in receiving timely updates on APHIS's Lacey Act efforts to register for our stakeholder registry at https://public.govdelivery.com/accounts/USDAAPHIS/subscriber/new and select "Lacey Act" as a topic of interest.

Scope of the Declaration Requirement

11. Which Products Need To Be Declared?

Currently, only items classified in certain HTS Chapters are scheduled for enforcement of the requirement to file a plant import declaration. Any changes to the current phase-in schedule will be announced in the *Federal Register*.

For the specific phase-in schedule, please consult: http://www.aphis.usda.gov/plant health/lacey act/downloads/ImplementationSchedule.pdf.

12. Does the Declaration Requirement Apply to All Types of Entries?

At present, we will be enforcing the declaration requirement for formal entries (i.e., most commercial shipments).

At this time, we are not requiring a declaration for informal entries (i.e., most personal shipments), personal importations, or mail, transportation and exportation entries, in-transit movements, carnet importations (i.e., merchandise or equipment that will be re-exported within a year), and foreign trade zone and warehouse entries. As with changes in the implementation schedule, we would issue a Federal Register notice before requiring a declaration for such imports.

13. What Is Considered Packaging Material, and Do I Have to Declare It?

For the purposes of the Lacey Act declaration requirement, packaging material is defined as any material used to support, protect, or carry another item.

This includes, but is not limited to, items such as: wood crating, wood pallets, cardboard boxes, packing paper used as cushioning, etc. Packaging material is exempt from the Lacey Act's declaration requirement unless the packaging material itself is the item being imported or it is used for some other purpose than supporting, protecting or carrying another item.

14. I Am Importing CITES Regulated Material That Already Has Proper CITES Documentation, Do I Need to Declare?

At this time, all shipments of material (including CITES regulated material) that fall under the sections of the HTS Chapters listed in the implementation schedule AND makes *formal customs entry* into the United States must be declared.

15. Is There an Exemption for Scientific Specimens?

Scientific specimens of plant genetic material (including roots, seeds, germplasm, parts, or products thereof) that are to be used only for laboratory or field research are excluded from the definition of "plant" unless they are listed in an appendix to CITES, as an endangered or threatened species under the Endangered Species Act, or pursuant to any State law that provides for the conservation of species that are indigenous to the State and are threatened with extinction.

16. One or More Components of My Merchandise Would Require a Declaration, but the Finished Product Does Not Fall within HTS Chapters Which Are Listed in the Implementation Schedule. Do I Need to Declare My Merchandise?

At this time, we plan to enforce the requirement of the plant import declaration only for those subchapters of HTS Chapters that appear in the implementation schedule published in the *Federal Register* on September 2, 2009.

The declaration requirement is based on the HTS code of the complete product being imported and not its component parts.

If your product does not fall on the implementation schedule, you do not have to submit a declaration. However, you must still exercise due care to ensure that the plant(s) or plant product(s) you are importing were legally harvested.

17. Will the Declaration Require Information on the "Chain of Custody" for Products or the Raw Materials Used to Manufacture The Products Being Imported?

No. The declaration will require information on the species of plant (the scientific name), the name of the country where the plant was taken (harvested), the value of the shipment and quantity of the plant material.

18. If I Genuinely Do Not Know the Species or the Country from Which the Plant Was Taken, Should I Guess?

No. In order to import plant products that fall under the scope of the declaration requirement, you are required to declare this information. However, the statute does provide that in the case in which the species of plant used to produce a plant product that is the subject of an importation varies, and the exact species used to produce the plant product is unknown, the declaration shall contain the name of each species of plant that may have been used to produce the plant product. Furthermore, in the case in which the species of plant used to produce a plant product that is the subject of an importation is commonly taken from more than one country, and the exact country from which the plant was taken and used to produce the product is unknown, the declaration shall contain the name of each country from which the plant may have been taken.

19. Which Countries Have Imports That Are Subject to the Provisions of the Lacey Act?

Imports from all countries are subject to the provisions of the Lacey Act. This includes imports of materials whose origin is the USA.

Filing a Declaration

20. What Agency/Office Will Collect the Information on the Declaration Forms?

The electronic declaration information will be collected by Customs and Border Protection, Department of Homeland Security. The paper declaration will be collected by Animal and Plant Health Inspection Service, United States Department of Agriculture.

21. When and Where Do I Declare My Merchandise?

The electronic declaration will be submitted through Customs Entry System via the Automated Broker Interface (ABI). This requires an updating of the third-party software used to submit Entry information. Please ensure that your software is up to date and the data entry requirements are met according to the_Customs and Trade Automated Interface Requirements (CATAIR).

If you make an electronic entry, and your merchandise falls under the Lacey Act declaration requirement; you will automatically be prompted to enter Lacey Act declaration information.

If you do not submit the Lacey Act declaration electronically and you are required to do so, then you must submit a paper declaration at the time of import.

22. What Is the Process for Submitting a Paper Declaration Form?

Go to the main page of the APHIS Lacey Act website at http://www.aphis.usda.gov/plant_health/lacey_act and fill out a copy of paper declaration form (PPQ Form 505).

Importers should have a copy of the form available for Customs and Border Protection (CBP) to review at the port of entry. After CBP clears the shipment, the importer must enter the entry number at the top of the form and mail the original form to USDA at the following address: The Lacey Act, c/o the US Department of Agriculture, Box 10, 4700 River Road, Riverdale, MD 20737.

23.What Is Meant by Entered Value (Section 12) of the Declaration Form?

Entered value is the value of the entire shipment in US dollars and is the same value used for Customs Entry.

24. What Is Meant by Unit of Measure (Section 17) of the Declaration Form?

The unit of measure is the unit that best describes the amount of declared plant material in a shipment (such as kilograms, meters, square meters, or cubic meters).

Only metric units will be accepted.

25. What Is Meant by Country of Harvest (Section 15) of the Declaration Form?

The country of harvest is the country where the original source material was grown, and subsequently cut down, picked, or otherwise removed (i.e., harvested). This may not be the same country that subsequently processed or is exporting the material. Thus, the country of harvest of the declared plant material may differ from the country of origin of the finished product.

26. Will Importers Be Permitted to Submit Blanket Declarations?

The current electronic system does not permit importers to file blanket declarations. As we move towards a more permanent system to collect and store Lacey Act declaration information, we will consider how to accommodate such declarations.

27. Will My Declaration Information Be Publicly Available?

Under US law certain information in the control of the government is by law publicly available through various channels.

The US Government has not made a formal decision on whether declaration information will be made publicly available outside of formal legal processes such as FOIA requests.

It is likely that at least some of the information will be made available to interested parties. Under existing legal frameworks, it is anticipated that any information provided to third parties will not contain identifying information for the importer, exporter, or consignee.

28. Who Is Responsible for Signing the Paper Declaration Form?

The Importer of Record is responsible for completing the declaration form, signing it, and submitting it to APHIS.

A Customs Broker can sign the Declaration form only if they have Power of Attorney for the Importer of Record, however, in doing so they take upon themselves the same legal responsibility for the accuracy of the information as they do when filing the regular entry data.

29. Do I Have to Declare Hand Carried Items Such as Passenger Baggage?

Currently, the declaration is only required for products imported into the United Sates as a Formal Entry.

Items in passenger baggage or personal items travelling with a person do not require a declaration.

For example, if you are travelling with your personal guitar, you are not required to declare the plant material in the guitar.

30. Do I Have To Declare Musical Instruments Coming from or Going to a Performance?

Musical Instruments transported for performance purposes do not require a declaration.

Only musical instruments being commercially imported as a Formal Consumption Entry would require a declaration.

Enforcement of the Declaration Requirement

31. What Is Considered Due Care with Respect to the Declaration Requirement of the Lacey Act?

The declaration requirement is specifically excluded from the "due care" penalty provisions under the Lacey Act.

Civil and criminal penalties apply only to any person who *knowingly* violates the declaration requirements.

In addition, any person who violates the declaration requirement, except for knowing violators, may be assessed a civil administrative penalty of $250.

Furthermore, any plant or plant product imported in violation of the import declaration requirements may be subject to forfeiture.

32. Is There an Innocent Owner Exception for Plants and Plant Products Imported in Violation of the Declaration Requirement?

No.

33. Will Shipments Be Refused Entry If the Information Required in the Declarations Is Not Known and Not Provided?

Shipments not in compliance with the law may be refused entry. Such enforcement decisions are made on a case-by-case basis, as with any other customs entry requirement violation.

34. The Lacey Act States That If the Species Contained in the Product Varies and the Actual Species Is Unknown, Then the Declaration Should "Contain the Name of the Species That May Have Been Used..." Can the Product Be Seized and/or Forfeited If I Am Wrong?

Yes. A product covered by the declaration requirements in the Lacey Act is subject to seizure and forfeiture if the declaration is inaccurate. However, as with any other customs declaration requirement violations, enforcement agencies may exercise discretion on any potential penalties depending upon the severity of the incident.

35. Will Third Party Certification Guarantee That Products Cannot Be Held Based on Suspicion of Illegality?

No. Although most certification systems for forest products include legality of harvest among their criteria, these are voluntary, private sector systems, the accuracy of which cannot be readily determined by the government.

Nevertheless, such certification systems may provide information useful to manufacturers and importers in their efforts to exercise due diligence regarding sources and species of timber.

36. The Lacey Act States That If the Species Used Commonly Comes from More Than One Country and the Actual Location of Harvest Is Unknown, Then the Declaration Should "Contain the Name of the Country from Which the Plant May Have Been Taken..." Can the Product Be Seized and/or Forfeited If I Am Wrong?

Yes. See Response to Question 31.

37. Will There Be an "Enforcement Plan?" Will Specific Countries/Products Be Targeted?

There will not be an "enforcement plan" with respect to the new provisions of the Lacey Act.

However, the new Lacey Act provisions (other than the declaration requirement) enacted as part of the 2008 Farm Bill are now effective, and responsible federal agencies fully intend to enforce these new provisions.

How enforcement resources will be allocated is yet to be determined; in general, enforcement priorities and plans are not discussed in detail.

In most enforcement work, if information is developed indicating a high likelihood of violations of a particular type, enforcement resources will likely focus on those types of activities.

38.How Soon Can We Expect Enforcement Actions Based on This New Authority? Are There Cases Currently under Investigation?

The new Lacey Act provisions are applicable to activities occurring on or after May 22, 2008.

Enforcement actions can be anticipated if and when there is legally sufficient evidence of a violation that was committed on or after that date.

It is government policy to neither confirm nor deny the existence of any particular criminal ongoing investigations.

39. Will Additional Resources Be Made Available for Enforcement? Will Additional Investigators and Prosecutors Be Hired?

Congress has not allocated any specific funds for the hiring of additional investigators or prosecutors to enforce the new provisions. Existing enforcement resources already are committed to enforcing the Lacey Act and will enforce the new provisions as well. Enforcement resources are regularly reassessed and reallocated to ensure their best use.

40. What Sources and/or Types of Information Will Be Used to Take Enforcement Actions? Will Enforcement Be Based on Information Provided by the Public?

As with other statutes, federal investigators and prosecutors make use of reliable information from a variety of sources in investigation and enforcement of the Lacey Act, including but not limited to information provided by members of the public.

41. What Are the Penalties for Violating the Amended Lacey Act?

Violations of the Lacey Act provisions for timber and other plants, as well as fish and wildlife, may be prosecuted in three basic ways:

- Civilly – meaning monetary penalties
- Criminally – fines and penalties and potential incarceration
- Forfeiture – dispossession of the plant, fish, or wildlife in question

Civil Penalties. The Lacey Act allows for the imposition of civil administrative monetary penalties against a party who in the exercise of due care should have known of the illegal nature of the plant or wildlife in question, or who knowingly commits a false labeling offense or knowingly violates the declaration requirements.

Civil penalties of up to $10,000 may be imposed, with the size of the penalty depending on the nature, circumstances, extent, and gravity of the prohibited act committed and the violator's culpability, ability to pay, and such other matters as justice may require. In addition, any person who commits a marking offense or violates the declaration requirements, except for knowing violators, may be assessed a penalty up to $250.

Criminal Penalties. Criminal penalties may also be imposed for certain violations, with the offense being either a felony or misdemeanor depending on, primarily, the defendant's knowledge, or mens rea, of the underlying illegality of the product at issue.

Misdemeanor. In order to impose a misdemeanor criminal penalty, the government must show that the defendant "in the exercise of due care" should have known of the illegal nature of the plant, fish, or wildlife in question, although not necessarily the specific law violated.

A defendant found guilty of a Lacey Act misdemeanor shall be fined not more than $100,000 for individuals or $200,000 for organizations, or imprisoned not more than one year, or both, for each violation.

Felony. In order to impose a felony criminal penalty, the government must show that the defendant "knew" or was generally aware of the illegal nature of the plant, fish, or wildlife, although not necessarily the specific law violated. Felony violations, in addition to a "knowing" scienter or mens rea requirement, require either proof that the defendant knowingly imported or exported plants or wildlife, or "knowingly" engaged in conduct during the offense that involved the sale or purchase of, the offer for sale or purchase of, or the intent to sell or purchase plants or wildlife with a market value of over $350.

A defendant found guilty of a Lacey Act felony shall be fined not more than $250,000 for individuals or $500,000 for organizations or twice the amount of the gross gain or loss, or imprisoned not more than 5 years, or both, for each violation.

Forfeiture. The Lacey Act's civil forfeiture provisions are enforced on a strict liability basis.

If illegal timber or a product made from illegal timber (and/or illegal wildlife or fish) is brought into the US, that timber or timber product may be seized whether or not the person from whom it is seized knew of the illegal nature of the product.

Nonetheless, the government must still show that a plant, plant product, or wildlife has been imported or received in violation of a State or foreign law or regulation.

Domestic Requirements and Interstate Movement

42. How Do the 2008 Amendments of the Lacey Act Apply to Forest, Farm and Associated Operations within the United States and Our Trust Territories?

The 2008 Farm Bill amended the Lacey Act by expanding its protection to a broader range of plants and plant products than were previously covered by the Act.

The Lacey Act now, among other things, makes it unlawful to import applicable timber or plant products without an import declaration (see other Q&A's specifically on the new declaration requirement).

The Lacey Act prohibitions against illegal harvest, transport and trade can also be prosecuted domestically in cases where covered timber and plants are illegally taken from Federal land, or illegally taken from State or private lands and then entered into interstate or foreign commerce.

Finally, the Lacey Act makes it unlawful to make or submit any false record or label with respect to any covered plant or plant product, including timber.

43. What Constitutes a Lacey Act Violation Based on Violation of Domestic Law?

Cases may include, but are not limited to, those involving the transportation, sale, receipt, acquisition or purchase of illegally taken plants, including timber.

Illegally taken plants are those plants taken in violation of Federal, State or Tribal law, including State forest practice acts.

Generally, Lacey Act violations are triggered when the illegally taken plants are entered into interstate or foreign commerce, or when such products are transported within or from Federal or Tribal lands.

Therefore, if a tree is illegally harvested in a national park, Lacey Act charges may be brought against any person who exports, transports (even if the transport remains within the same Federal jurisdiction), sells, receives, or purchases that tree, timber from the tree, or any product thereof.

44. Is New Documentation Now Required for the Interstate Transport of Timber and Plant Products?

No. Although the Lacey Act does now require an import declaration for timber and plant products being imported into the United States, it does not introduce any new documentation requirement for interstate transport of plants or plant products. However, if the product leaves the United States and is imported back at a later date, it would have to abide by the import requirements of the Act as well, including the declaration requirement.

45. Does the Amendment Apply to or Affect Management of Domestic Forest Operations or the Reporting Requirements Associated with Them?

The prohibitions of the amended Lacey Act apply to domestic (interstate) commerce as well as international trade (both imports and exports). The amended Lacey Act does not require anything explicitly different or additional of forest operations, nor does it impose any additional paperwork or reporting requirements beyond the new import declaration. However, those responsible for a variety of plant and timber transport, purchasing and processing should know their supply sources as a matter of good practice. Those who either knowingly or unknowingly accept illegally taken and transported covered plant or timber products may be subject to prosecution and/or loss of the shipment due to seizure and forfeiture (see relevant Q&As on penalties and enforcement actions associated with the Lacey Act). US exporters of a plant or timber that is finished internationally and imported back into the US may need to provide species and country of harvest information so that the subsequent importer can comply with their declaration requirements.

46. What Additional Tools or Options Does the Lacey Act Potentially Provide for Dealing with Domestic Timber Theft That Did Not Exist Before?

Illegally taken timber and plant products can now be seized/forfeited and those who do not exercise due care in the procurement, purchase and transport of such products can be prosecuted under the Lacey Act if the plant products were illegally harvested on Federal or Tribal land, or if they were illegally harvested in violation of State law and entered into interstate commerce. Therefore, the amended Lacey Act now provides the basis for greater cooperation among States, and between the States and the Federal government to combat timber theft. States can now work with the appropriate Federal law enforcement agencies to investigate and prosecute Lacey Act violations. For further information, please see the Q&A's on the enforcement provisions of the Lacey Act.

47. Will Federal Agents Be "Checking" Compliance with State Forest Practices Regulations?

State forest practices regulations are enforced by their respective State jurisdictions. However, in cases where illegally taken plant products are transported across State lines, involved States can now cooperate with the federal prosecutors to bring Federal Lacey Act charges against violators. It is possible that information obtained by or provided to Federal agents may lead to Federal Lacey Act charges against violators of State forest and plant conservation laws and regulations.

48. Does The Lacey Act Apply Differently to Timber Harvested in Violation of Federal, State or Tribal Law?

Yes. On State and private lands, the Lacey Act prohibits the transportation, sale, receipt, acquisition, or purchase in interstate or foreign commerce of covered plants, timber or plant products harvested in violation of State conservation laws and regulations. On Federal and Tribal lands and jurisdiction, the same prohibitions apply regardless of whether the plant, timber or product was entered into interstate or foreign commerce.

49. What Federal Agencies Will Be Responsible for Enforcing the Lacey Act Domestically?

In cases where timber and other plant products are illegally taken from Federal land, the designated Federal law enforcement agency (i.e. US Forest Service, National Park Service, US Fish and Wildlife Service, etc.) has enforcement authority. For cases involving State and private land, there is currently no single Federal enforcement agency or clearly established processes or agency relationships. The Forest Service is currently exploring this issue and possible alternatives.

In: The Lacey Act
Editors: G. E. Morgan and D. Hill ISBN 978-1-62081-615-8

Chapter 4

LACEY ACT PRIMER*

The United States Department of Agriculture Animal and Plant Health Inspection Service

HISTORY OF THE LACEY ACT

- Oldest wildlife protection statute in the US
- It was first enacted in 1900 to combat impact of:
  - hunting to supply commercial markets
  - interstate shipment of unlawfully killed game
  - introduction of harmful exotic species
  - killing of birds for feather trade
- Significantly amended in 1981 and 1988
- Amended again in 2008
- A tool to combat trafficking in "illegal"
- wildlife, fish or plants

The 2008 Farm Bill (the Food, Conservation and Energy Act of 2008)

- Section 8204. Prevention of Illegal Logging Practices expands Lacey protection to broader range of plants

---

* This is an edited, reformatted and augmented version of The United States Department of Agriculture, Animal and Plant Health Inspection Service publication, dated April 2010.

- Now encompasses products, including timber, derived from illegally harvested plants
- New declaration requirement for plant products
- Effective May 22, 2008

PURPOSE OF THE LACEY ACT AMENDMENT

- Prevent trade in illegally harvested lumber
- Prevent trade in wood products made from illegally harvested lumber

THE LACEY ACT MAKES IT ...

- Unlawful to trade in any plant that is taken, possessed, transported, or sold in violation of the laws of the United States, a State, Indian Tribe, or any foreign law that protects plants.
  - Applies to interstate and foreign commerce
- Unlawful to falsify or submit falsified documents, accounts or records of any plant covered by the Act
- Unlawful to import certain plants and plant products without an import declaration

IN PLAIN ENGLISH ...

- Make sure your shipments were obtained legally
- Make sure your shipments' documentation and records are true and accurate
- Make sure your shipment is properly declared under the Lacey Act declaration requirement

Full text available in the Federal Register Docket No. APHIS-2008-0119

Phase-in schedule of enforcement of the declaration requirement for goods of, or containing, plants or plant products*

Phase II April 1, 2009	Phase III October 1, 2009	Phase IV April 1, 2010
FITS Chapters:	H'I'S Chapters:	Fur s Chapters:
Ch. 44 Headings (wood & articles of wood)	Ch. 44 Headings (wood & articles of wood)	Ch. 44 Headings (wood & articles of wood)
• 4401--(Fuel wood)	• 4402—Wood charcoal	• 4421—Other articles of wood
• 4403—(Wood in the rough)	• 4412—Plywood, veneered panels	
• 4404—Hoopwood; poles, piles, stakes)	o except 44129906 and 44129957 • 4414—Woodenframes	Ch. 66 Headings (umbrellas, walking sticks, riding crops)
• 4406—Railway or tramway sleepers) • 4407—(Wood sawn or chipped lengthwise)	• 4419—Tableware & kitchenware of wood	• 6602—Walking sticks, whips, crops
• 4408—(Sheets for veneering)	• 4420—Wood marquetry, caskets, statuettes.	
• 4409—(Wood continuously shaped)		
• 4417—(Tools, tool handles, broom handles)		Ch. 82 Headings (tools, implements)
• 4418—(Builders' joinery and carpentry of wood).		• 8201—Hand tools
		Ch. 92 Headings (musical instruments)
		• 9201—Pianos

Phase-in schedule of enforcement … (Continued)

Phase II April 1, 2009	Phase III October 1, 2009	Phase IV April 1, 2010
		• 9202—Other stringed instruments
		Ch. 93 Headings (arms and ammunition)
		• 9302—Revolvers and pistols
		• 93051020—Parts and accessories for re-volvers and pistols
		Ch. 94 Headings (f umiture etc.)
		• 940169—Seats with wood frames
		Ch. 95 Headings (toys, games, & sporting equipment)
		• 950420—Articles and accessories for billiards
		Ch. 97 Headings (works of art)
		• 9703—Sculptures
	PLUS PHASES II	PLUS PHASES II & III

* Declaration requirements were effective as of l)ecem berl 5, 2008. All declarations submitted mast he accurate; false statements may he referred for enforcement. Failure to submit a declaration will not be prosecuted, and customs clearance will not be denied for lack of a declaration until after the phase-in date above.

EXEMPTIONS FROM THE DECLARATION REQUIREMENT

- Currently only sections of HTS Chapters 44, 66, 82, 92, 93, 94, 95 & 97 are scheduled for enforcement of the declaration requirement
- Plants and plant products used exclusively as packing material to support, protect, or carry another item including (but not limited to):Instruction manuals, labels, pallets and crating, etc.
- "Common cultivars" and "common food crops"
  - To be defined by APHIS and FWS in joint rulemaking
- Plants for planting

LACEY ACT VS. DECLARATION REQUIREMENT

- The Declaration Requirement is only a small part of the entire Lacey Act
- Even if a shipment is exempt from the Declaration Requirement –the Lacey Act is still in force
- Example: Bagpipes with wooden pipes
  - HTS Section 92059020 –no declaration required
  - The Lacey Act itself still applies to the wooden pipes
  - If the pipes were made from illegally harvested treesthen the bagpipe shipment is in violation of the Lacey Act

LACEY ACT VIOLATIONS AND PENALTIES

- Forfeiture –strict liability
- Misdemeanors punishable by 1 year in prison and a fine of $ 100,000 ($200,000 for corporations)
  - In the exercise of due care, individual/corporation should have known the plant was illegally taken, possessed, transported or sold
  - Was aware of illegality, but the incident did not involve import or export or commercial conduct with plant value of more than $350
  - Applicable only to substantive violations, NOT to declaration requirements

- Felonies punishable by 5 years in prison and a $250,000 fine ($500,000 for corporations)
  - Knowing violation –knowledge of facts and illegality, not specific law violated
  - Involves import or export or commercial conduct with plant value of more than $350

Enforcement Basics

- Fact based, not document based
- Government burden to prove to a jury of defendant's peers
- Information gained from
  - Foreign governments
  - NGOs
  - Private citizens
  - Anonymous tips
  - Data analysis -declarations
  - Industry members –whistle blowers & competitors
  - Agents on the border
- The Federal Government will always evaluate and substantiate initial information before launching full investigation
- Enforcement/investigating agencies include USFWS, ICE, CBP, APHIS, USDA OIG, FBI, USFS

Due Care

- Ninth Circuit Pattern Jury Instructions
  - "Due care means that degree of care which a reasonably prudent person would exercise under the same or similar circumstances."
- Legislative History
  - "Due care simply requires that a person facing a particular set of circumstances undertakes certain steps which a reasonable man would take to do his best to insure that he is not violating the law."

- Due care "is applied differently to different categories of persons with varying degrees of knowledge and responsibility.
- For example, zoo curators, as professionals, are expected to apply their knowledge to each purchase of wildlife. If they know that a reptile is Australian and that Australia does not allow export of that reptile without special permits, they would fail to exercise due care unless they check for those permits.
- On the other hand, the airline company which shipped the reptile might not have the expertise to know that Australia does not normally allow that particular reptile to be exported. However, if an airline is notified of the problem and still transships the reptile, then it would probably fail to pass the due care test."

Tools to Demonstrate Due Care

- Asking questions
- Compliance plans
- Industry standards
- Records of efforts
- Changes in above in response to practical experiences

Some Examples of Common-Sense Red Flags

- Goods significantly below going market rate
- Cash only/lower price for goods without paperwork
- Paperwork facially invalid or otherwise suspect
- Unusual sales methods or practices
- Transactions fit the description of illegal transactions discussed in trade/industry publications
- Inability of suppliers to provide rational answers to routine questions

Other Lacey Act Basics

- The underlying foreign law violation does not have to be a criminal violation, nor one actively enforced in the foreign country.

- The underlying violation need not be committed by the person charged with violating the Lacey Act –a third party might have taken the product illegally.
- The underlying foreign law can be interpreted by US Courts

TAXONOMY AND SCIENTIFIC NAMES

- Kingdom
- – Phylum
- Class
- – Order
- ✓ Family
- ✓ Genus
- ✓ Species

Example: Red Oak

• Kingdom	• Plantae
– Phylum	– Magnoliophyta
• Class	• Rosopsida
– Order	– Fagales
✓ Family	✓ Fagaceae
✓ Genus	✓ Quercus
✓ Species	✓ rubra

Quercus Rubra

I DO DECLARE ...

- Paper Declaration Process
- Electronic Declaration Process
- Blanket Declaration Process

Sample Declaration

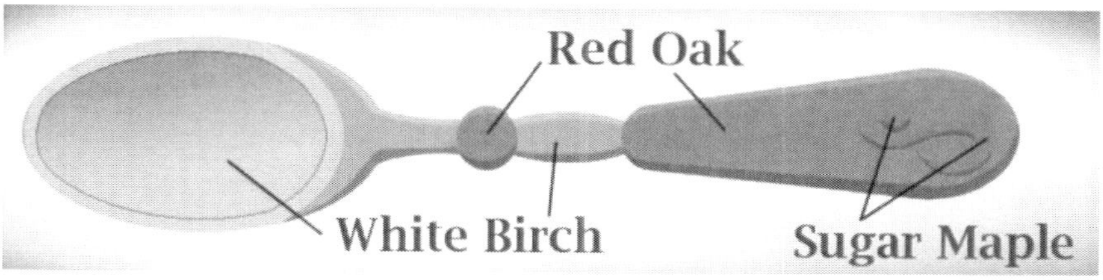

- Make two copies of the Declaration, Mail one copy to APHIS
- Send other copy with shipment/documentation for CBP
- Envelope opened, importer noted, determination whether new, resubmitted, or Estimate.
- Declaration vetted for accuracy and compliance.
- Importer contacted if vetting reveals errors.
- Declaration entered into Excel by Data Entry Personnel.
- Entered data quality checked for completeness and accuracy.
- Data moved into master database.
- Analysis, etc.
- Paper declarations archived for 6 years.

Paper Declarations –How to? (Part 1)

- Download the PDF PPQ505 from the APHIS site
  - Save it to your computer hard drive
- Read the instructions
  - Pages 3 and 4
- Filling out the Declaration
  - Print out the PDF and fill the form by hand,

    or,
  - Fill in the PDF form using Acrobat, then print it out.

Paper Declarations -Other

- Use Box 10 "Description of Merchandise"
  - CITES Material

SECTION 1 - Shipment Information

1. ESTIMATED DATE OF ARRIVAL: (MM/DD/YYYY) 09/23/2009	
2. ENTRY NUMBER: ENT-0000000-0	3. CONTAINER NUMBER: CONT00000000
4. BILL OF LADING: 0000000	5. MID: MID000000000
6. IMPORTER NAME: Importer Name	8. CONSIGNEE NAME: Consignee Name
7. IMPORTER ADDRESS: 000 Importer Rd Importer, IM 00000	9. CONSIGNEE ADDRESS: 000 Consignee Rd Consignee, CE 00000

I certify under penalty of perjury that the information furnished is true and correct:

Johnny Importer	Johnny Importer	09/12/2009
Signature	Type or Print Name	Date

Knowingly making a false statement in this Declaration for Importation may subject the declarant to criminal penalties in accordance with 16 U.S.C. 3373(d).

SECTION 2 - Compliance with Lacey Act Requirements (16 U.S.C. 3372(f))

10. DESCRIPTION OF MERCHANDISE: 1,250 Decorative Wooden Spoons	11. HTSUS NUMBER: (no dashes/symbols) 44190040 ☐ See Attachment 12. ENTERED VALUE: (in U.S. Dollars) 1,000,000,000

For each article or component of an article, provide the following:

13. ARTICLE/ COMPONENT OF ARTICLE	14. PLANT SCIENTIFIC NAME: (Genus and Species)	15. COUNTRY OF HARVEST:	16. QUANTITY OF PLANT MATERIAL:	17. UNIT OF MEASURE:	18. % RECYCLED MATERIAL:
Red Oak handle – 1.2" x 2.3"	Quercus rubra	Canada	0.0426	m3	0
Red Oak handle – 1.2" x 2.3"	Quercus rubra	USA	0.0106	m3	0
Red Oak knob – 1.2" x 1.2"	Quercus rubra	Canada	0.1482	m3	0
White Birch bowl – 3" x 4.2"	Betula pubescens	Russian Federation	5.161	m3	0
White Birch tang – 0.75" x 5"	Betula pubescens	Russian Federation	0.0452	m3	0
Sugar Maple inlay – 0.1" thick	Acer saccharum	Guatemala	0.132	kg	0
	Acer saccharum	USA	0	kg	0
	Acer saccharum	Canada	0	kg	0
	Acer saccharum	Mexico	0	kg	0

- Enter CITES Permit Number
  - Goods Manufactured Prior to Amendment
- Enter "Manufactured Prior to May 22, 2008"
  - For material that cannot be identified mark the Genus as "Special" and mark the species as "PreAmendment"
  - Musical Instruments for performances

- Enter "Musical Instruments for use in performance" or,
- Enter "Musical Instruments returning from performance"

Electronic Declaration

- Declaration entered into Customs Automated Broker Interface (ABI).
- CBP provides APHIS with declarations.
- Data converted to Excel format.
- Declarations vetted for accuracy and compliance.
- Importer contacted if vetting reveals errors.
- Data moved into master database.
- Analysis, etc.
- Future data in ACE?

Electronic Declarations – How to? (Part 1)

- Electronic Declarations
  - Aresubmitted directly to USCBP via ABI
  - Requirere-programming of the broker software
  - Havea veryspecific dataset and formatting requirements
- Electronic Declarations are NOTmadevia a website
  - via PDF
  - Via email

Electronic Declarations – How to? (Part 2)

- Introducing the CATAIR*
- See the CBP website: http://www.cbp.gov/xp/cgov/trade/automated/automated_systems/abi/catair/user_requirements.xml
- PGA Datasets
- Contact your Customs Client Representative for any questions regarding the CATAIR

Electronic Declarations –How to? (Part 3)

Record Identifier PG05 (Input)					
	Length/ Cla				
Data Element		Position	Status	Description	Note
	ss				
Control Identifier	2A	1-2	M	Must always equal PG.	
Record Type	2N	3-4	M	Must always be 05.	
				Scientific Genus Name of the PGA's merchandise	
*Scientific Genus Name	22A	5-26	C	Being entered.	
*Scientific Species	22A	27-48	C	Scientific Species Name of the PGA's merchandise	
Name				being entered.	
Scientific Sub Species	18A	49-66	C	Scientific Sub SpeciesName of the PGA's	
Name				merchandise being entered.	
Scientific Species Code	7AN	67-73	C	This includes Fish and Wildlife Service (FWS) Wildlife	
				Category codes.	
FWS Description Code	7AN	74-80	C	FWS Description Codes assigned by FWS.	

Example: PG05pinus radiata

Blanket Declaration

- Only open to certain group of importers (currently BRASS and ALR participants)
- Importer applies for membership to program.
- Application reviewed.
- Importer mails Estimated 505 by 1stof month to be declared.
- Importer sends Excel spreadsheet of reconciled data by 15ththe following month.

- Declarations vetted for accuracy and compliance.
- Importer contacted if vetting reveals errors.
- Data moved into master database.
- Analysis, etc.
- Applications, Estimates, etc. archived.

SUGGESTED BEST PRACTICES

- Ask your overseas supplier for Genus/species
- Check botanical resources (e.g. GRIN Taxonomy)
  - Confirm validity of scientific names
  - Confirm geographic distribution
- Check with Foreign Government Authorities
  - Confirm source companies operate legally (licensed/certified)
  - Request pertinent plant protection laws (country of harvest)
- Keep complete records of your efforts
- When in doubt –Call APHIS!

APHIS LACEY ACT WEBSITE

http://www.aphis.usda.gov/plant_health/lacey_act/index.shtml

WHAT YOU WILL FIND THERE ...

- Link to PPQ Form 505: Plant and Plant Product Declaration Form
- Links to Lacey Act Federal Register Notices
- Links to other Lacey Act related Documents
- Link to look up for plant genus and species
- Link to Lacey Act Declaration email address
- Link to PPQ Stakeholder Registry

Please refer Lacey Act inquiries to: lacey.act.declaration@aphis.usda.gov

INDEX

A

B

C

INDEX

G

H

I

J

K

L

M

N

O

P